RockaSocka

A Musical Play

John Gardiner

A Samuel French Acting Edition

SAMUELFRENCH-LONDON.CO.UK
SAMUELFRENCH.COM

Copyright © 1992 by John Gardiner (Book and Lyrics)
All Rights Reserved

ROCKASOCKA is fully protected under the copyright laws of the British Commonwealth, including Canada, the United States of America, and all other countries of the Copyright Union. All rights, including professional and amateur stage productions, recitation, lecturing, public reading, motion picture, radio broadcasting, television and the rights of translation into foreign languages are strictly reserved.

ISBN 978-0-573-08091-3

www.samuelfrench-london.co.uk

www.samuelfrench.com

FOR AMATEUR PRODUCTION ENQUIRIES

UNITED KINGDOM AND WORLD EXCLUDING NORTH AMERICA

plays@SamuelFrench-London.co.uk

020 7255 4302/01

Each title is subject to availability from Samuel French, depending upon country of performance.

CAUTION: Professional and amateur producers are hereby warned that *ROCKASOCKA* is subject to a licensing fee. Publication of this play does not imply availability for performance. Both amateurs and professionals considering a production are strongly advised to apply to the appropriate agent before starting rehearsals, advertising, or booking a theatre. A licensing fee must be paid whether the title is presented for charity or gain and whether or not admission is charged.

The professional rights in this play are controlled by Samuel French Ltd, 52 Fitzroy Street, London, W1T 5JR.

No one shall make any changes in this title for the purpose of production. No part of this book may be reproduced, stored in a retrieval system, or transmitted in any form, by any means, now known or yet to be invented, including mechanical, electronic, photocopying, recording, videotaping, or otherwise, without the prior written permission of the publisher. No one shall upload this title, or part of this title, to any social media websites.

The right of John Gardiner to be identified as author of this work has been asserted by him in accordance with Section 77 of the Copyright, Designs and Patents Act 1988

CHARACTERS

Sheba Shekelstein, chairwoman of City F.C. Heiress to the Shekelstein Swimwear & Corset Empire, and owner of The Flamenco Da Gropa Dance Academy
Benny Shekelstein, her husband
Sylv Shekelstein, Sheba and Benny's daughter. She loves animals, footballers, and Gazza
Norbert, coach and trainer
Daphne Vestal, City F.C. Secretary
Joe Rabbit, Tea boy and Superstar

The City Football Team
All male roles

Shaky, Goalkeeper
Enid, Defence
Einstein, Defence
Titch, Attack
Lofty, Mid-field, Captain
Tubs, Attack

The City Opposition Team
All female roles. The same six girls play the individual team members

Bruddersford United
1. I. Wrench (Goalkeeper)
2. A. Brute (Defence)
3. V. Hement (Defence)
4. U. Butcher (Mid-field)
5. G.B.H. Hawkins (Attack)
6. D. Form (Striker)

Beaujolais Rangers
1. Claude Massif (Goalkeeper)
2. Marcel Wavette (Defence)
3. Stan Ackroyd (Defence—on loan)
4. Pasture de Midi (Mid-field)
5. Marcel Morceau (Attack)
6. Denise Defarge (Knitter)

Chi Hua Hua Academicals
1. Boleros Giganticus (Goalkeeper)
2. Tijuana Brasso (Defence)
3. Nasty Juarez (Defence)
4. Grandios Moustachios (Attack)
5. Midios D'Alfafa (Mid-field)
6. Big Maracas (Star)

This show requires six principals, six male characters for City Football team, six female characters/dancers to play all the opposition teams and a minimum of twenty-five to play the remaining characters.

The following roles can be doubled and trebled

Ground staff
Supporters
St John's Ambulance
Policeman and woman
Mrs Brillo, changing-room cleaner
Mrs Rinse, changing-room cleaner
Six shower girls
Air France personnel
Maurice le Fleur, manager of The Beaujolais Rangers
Herr Vistlekraut, the referee*
Air France Pilot
Queen
Golden Ball TV Floor Manager
Golden Ball TV Outside Broadcast Commentator
Fairies
Compere at the "Flamenco Da Gropa" ballroom
Da Gropa singers
Da Gropa ballroom dancers
Presidente Tequila of Mexico
Presidente's Right Hand Hombre

*In the original production the part of the referee was played by Benny Shekelstein using very fast costume changes but your production will be just as effective if the referee is cast as a distinct and separate character. The fairies were very young children (average age 7–9) from a local ballet school.

The action of the play takes place in various exterior and interior settings

Time—the present

ACT I, First Half The Ground
        Boardroom of City F.C.
        Training Pitch of City F. C.
        Changing-room and showers
        Sheba Shekelstein's private
         office
        London airport
        Paris
        The "Stade de Fromage"
         home of Beaujolais Rangers

Half Time

ACT II, Second Half Wembley Stadium
        Golden Ball Television Studio
        Flamenco Da Gropa dance
         hall
        Aztec stadium, home of Chi
         Hua Hua Academicals

MUSICAL NUMBERS

ACT I

1	City	All
1a	Music during announcements and entry of teams	
2	She's Gorn and Thrown a Wobbly	Sheba, Benny, Norbert, Sylv and Daphne
3	A Little Bit of Me	Joe and Sylv
3a	Hokey Cokey	Team
4	Muscle-Hustle	Sheba, Benny, Norbert and Team
4a	Entrance of Mrs Brillo and Mrs Rinse	
4b	Strip Streak Flasher	
5	Sortin' Out the Socks on Saturday	Mrs Rinse and Mrs Brillo
5b	Musica Romantica	
6	A Little Bit of Me (Reprise)	Joe and Sylv
7	City (Reprise)	Supporters
7a	Music during announcements and entry of teams	
7b	Hokey Cokey	City Team
7c	Airport chimes	
7d	French cafe music	
7e	Entrance of Beaujolais Rangers	
8	Maurice le Fleur	Beaujolais Rangers and Maurice le Fleur
8a	Land of Hope and Glory	
9	But We'll Support Yer (City reprise)	Supporters

ACT II

9b	When You Walk on a Frog	Joe and Supporters
10	Right Royal Occasion	Supporters and Teams
10a	Entrance of H.M. Queen	
10b	Exit of H.M. Queen	
11	Believe in Fairies	Daphne, Fairies and Joe Rabbit

11a	Swirling to the Ball	
11b	"City's are Red..."	City Team
11c	Music under "City, My City" documentary	
12	Smack it in the Back of the Net	City Team, Floor Manager and Opposition
12a	Music under compere's introduction	
12b	Fanfares	
13	The Valse Shekelstein	Singers
13b	Jezebel Tango	
14	Forgive Me, Already	Sheba
14a	Mexican Music	
15	Big Maracas	Hombres and Presidente
15a	Hokey Cokey	Chi Hua Hua
15b	Mexican Final—end of first half	
15c	The Fairies reappear	
16	Believe in Fairies (Reprise)	Fairies
16a	Tension Mounts	
17	Finale	Supporters
18	City (Reprise)	Supporters

The Set

The musical can be played on (1), a proscenium stage (2) in the round or (3), a thrust stage. In the original production it was played in the round. This consisted of a green, fully-marked, football pitch with the audience sitting on the 'terraces' either side. It is important to establish the audience as the football crowd so you would find that settings (2) or (3) make for the more exciting arena style as well as creating a sense of the 'big match' atmosphere. The football pitch can either be expensive plastic grass or simply a painted floorcloth. There are two mini goals with nets and either end of the pitch raised up are two huge red and white signs displaying the logo CITY F.C. Mock-up floodlights (using large tin cans painted black with bulb fittings) can also be very effective if placed in each corner above the pitch.

So that basically, the floor of your theatre, hall or studio is the pitch and the audience (preferably raked) are the City F.C. supporters.

In the case of a proscenium stage production the same set is used but the goals should be designed in perspective and placed SR and SL. The cyclorama may be used to fly or project the City F.C. symbol. Other symbols or cut-outs can be utilised to create the required atmosphere of particular scenes.

Whichever style of staging you use the set will be incredibly cheap and allows maximum space for dancing and action. The pace of the show is fast so avoid anything that creates clutter. Individual scenes are played on the pitch when furniture and props are set and struck by the actors.

Playing the arena

If you decide to play the show in the round you may find that there is sometimes an apprehension in the minds of less experienced actors created by the fact that they find that sometimes they are playing with their backs to the audience. They are unaware that the audience are seeing a picture rather than individuals. Put their minds at rest by repeating the fact the audience are at a football match and used to seeing the players backs. Stage directions can often be given as figures on a clock face rather than end stage phrases. So that upstage Centre would be 12 o'clock. Stage left becomes 3 o'clock, Down stage centre-6 and Stage right-9.

The Ball

The balls used in the show were cheap plastic. It is sensible to have a supply of match balls in access areas.

Aggro Bags
When the audience take their seats they should find a paper bag marked "Aggro Bag CITY F.C." either on or under their seats. The bag should contain paper missiles, old cartons, toilet rolls etc. It can be handy to ask every member of the cast to bring a toilet roll to cut down on expense! This can be used again and again after the Interval clean-up.

The bags are used in the pitch invasion at the end of Act One.

Programme

In the original production, the show programme was designed so that when opened it could be used as a City F.C. supporter's scarf.

Raffle

Have the World Cup Final Match Ball, signed by all the CITY F.C. players, raffled or give it away with a lucky programme number drawn at the end of the First Act. The winner may collect the ball from Joe Rabbit at the end of the show! It is sensible to have a duplicate ball already signed to save time.

The Football Matches

The matches should be carefully planned and choreographed. There are some guidelines and some suggestions of comic business that can be incorporated into the games. You will find that using the effects of slow motion and freeze for the action and the scoring of the goals allows the audience an opportunity of following the events clearly. These guidelines have been included in the text of the show. Individual performers should use their character to invent certain comic sequences. The referee is a lunatic and has a large 'Adolf Hitler' moustache—in the original show Benny Shekelstein played this role with hilarious changes of costume and character. He is officious and Germanic.

Supporters

Should be used to sell programmes and also argue about the strengths and weaknesses of the City team and the management. They can be utilised to intermingle with the audience in and around the foyer to create an atmosphere of pre-match fervour. They should play these 'impros' for real—very serious and genuinely concerned about City's future.

The Rhythmic Clap

Nearly all football supporters and followers are *au fait* with the chants and claps utilised at soccer matches—for the uninitiated the time sequence has been included in the text. You can of course adapt and use your own clap sequence or chant.

City F.C.

The show can either be played with the central heroes as City F.C. or you can substitute your own local side. Obviously the local amateur side would be best especially if they are not having a particularly good season. Contact your local club secretary—he can be very helpful with kit, publicity and ticket sales. Their lucky number programme prize could be two tickets for your production of "RockaSocka".

Local trade

Contact local sports outfitters, ice cream and peanut vendors and see what help they can give with free or cut price offers for Front of House sales.

Turnstiles

You might be able to use some kind of turnstile system in a simple but effective way to help your atmosphere by placing them at the entrance to the performing arena. They would have to be removed later to prevent any Fire precaution irregularity.

Busker

Before the match starts it is a good idea to have a busker, or one-man band or a proper band playing in the centre of the pitch to set the atmosphere. If you cannot provide live music then by all means use taped brass bands playing well-known tunes. The atmosphere when the audience arrive should be noisy and exciting.

Updating

Directors will almost certainly need to update certain names, sporting heroes and events within the text to give their production a fresh, contemporary humour. Please feel free to make such alterations and additions.

PRODUCTION NOTES

Characters and their costumes

The following costume list gives ideas upon which directors may expand.

Sheba Shekelstein—her costume should be opulent but tasteless. Opening scene—skirt, brightly coloured silk blouse with jabot, blue rinse wig, fur or leopard skin coat. Training scene: bright leisure jogging suit, trainers, sweat bands. Seduction scene: see script. France: bright trouser suit, chiffon neck scarf, dark glasses. Queen: two piece outfit with large hat, white gloves etc. Tango: see script. Mexico: holiday going away outfit—suggest Bermuda shorts, Hawaiian top, Mexican hat, sandals.

Benny Shekelstein—opening scene: large coat with velvet lapels (camel hair or blue) over dark baggy suit, white shirt and crooked tie. Training scene—filthy scruffy tracksuit. Other scenes as for opening but a hat when meeting the Queen. Mexico: as Sheba.

Sylv Shekelstein—her costumes should be pretty, fashionable and tasteful. Opening scene: fashionable casual wear with T-shirt top for GAZZA. The hamster should actually move. Song number: towelling bath wrap and towel for head, bare feet. France: a pretty casual going away outfit. Queen: as for Sheba. Other scenes: a pretty leisure jogging-suit with trainers.

Norbert—for all scenes a baggy track suit with trainers and flat caps. For tango scene see script.

Joe Rabbit—opening scene—jeans, trainers, T-shirt, white lab coat marked City F.C. (Catering) on back of coat. Wembley—white suit, shoes, white shirt. Fairies—all-in-one Rabbit suit (This can be hired from Richard Rosendale, Harlequin Costumes, Baldock, Herts or any major London costumier.) Other scenes: Red Shirt (marked Joe Rabbit on back), white shorts, red socks, trainers. Track suit marked City F.C.

Daphne Vestal—long skirt, wrinkled stockings, flat shoes, huge misshapen jumper, knitted tam-o'-shanter in City's colours, glasses. She should be unattractive. From "fairies" onwards fur coat, high heels covering the grot below.

The City Team—the red shirts, white shorts, red socks and trainers of City F.C. Each shirt should have the player's name printed on the back. The letters can be purchased and ironed on. Titch's shorts should come nearly down to his ankles. Enid's shorts should be brief with lace around the edges, while Tubs might need padding in his shirt. Lofty's shirt looks too small and Einstein has got his shirt on back to front. Shaky has a gigantic sweater that trails over his knees and a white stick and dark glasses. Shaky wears a broken down pair of suede boots, not trainers. All have tracksuits marked City F.C. on the back except Shaky. All have briefs marked City Supporters.

The Opposition Team (Dancers) **Bruddersford**—large padded shirts with shorts. Names on back optional. Black a few eyes, take out a few teeth add a few pieces of elastoplast on cheeks and the remnants of old injuries. The girls should look tough and act tough. Their socks have holes in.
Beaujolais—pretty football shirts, natty shorts, little berets that can be firmly pinned to the head—if in doubt dispense with berets in the dance number. Coloured socks.
TV Scene Pretty casual sport shirt tops with pretty shorts. Long white socks and white plimsolls.
Chi Hua Hua Bright shirts, shorts, socks, trainers but all must have Mexican moustaches—either crepe hair firmly fixed or pencilled in with greasestick. Vary the style of the moustache according to the character. Tijuana Brassos should be identical.

The Queen—look at pictures of Her Majesty and copy.

Referee—black shirt and shorts, one sock up the other down, Hitler moustache.

Fairies—keep them very young and if possible vary the size from tall down to very small. Tu-tus, tights and ballet shoes (flats—your local dance school will be able to help)

Maurice Le Fleur—as for Maurice Chevalier i.e. striped blazer, white or pink silk shirt, cravat, white trousers, white shoes, boater, cane.

Presidente Tequila—military uniform—see script. Grey or blue gaberdine. Peaked hat, riding crop, riding boots. Tank is merely hardboard or cardboard around supermarket trolley with gun extending. Tequila can push this on himself. Hombres can strike it.

Hombres—keep Supporters' gear on underneath squares of striped material with holes cut in centre. These will go over head and shoulders as Mexican capes, old, battered Mexican hats, Mexican moustaches. When changing back to Supporters at end of show, simply remove hat, pull or rub off moustache and remove cape. If you use guns these can be cut out of card larger than life, very funny e.g. barrels pointing up, down and sideways and painted. These would be used in execution and killing of Ardiles. Right Hand Hombre should be dressed the same but have a real gun and a throat-spray that he uses for Tequila's word problems. He will have to make the squirting noise orally—otherwise it will not carry to the back of the auditorium. The first Chi Hua Hua team are a group of Hombres. They do not dress in football kit.

Mrs Brillo and Mrs Rinse—charladies, flat shoes, wrinkled lisle stockings, skirts, shirt tops covered by wrap round apron overall, hair in curlers, head scarves, buckets, packet of pills. Two football outfits in City colours. Mrs Rinse has pair of large bloomers for her indecent exposure.

Da Gropa Compere—Evening dress suit with bow tie. Hair slicked down.

TV Floor Manager—"Medallion man". Green or turquoise frilled shirt open at the chest, medallion, frilled cuffs, blonde hair or wig, very tight lurex trousers, shoes to match, rings, clipboard, pencil.

Dancers at Da Gropa—see script.

Singers—men in tails, women in long black Victorian dresses with pince-nez and long hanging black jet beads. Hair should be up. Men's hair parted in the middle and slicked down.

Big Maracas—see script.

Groundstaff—wear plastic $\frac{3}{4}$ length tops or tabards with City F.C. printed on back, flat caps, jeans, boots etc. Turn these inside out for Beaujolais scene when they should have Beaujolais printed on the back. There are some reversible jackets like this on the market—but to keep costs down just mock up old Oxfam coats and cut to size.

Supporters—really aggressive, bovver boots, ripped vests, tattoos, jeans etc. City scarves can be made from cutting lengths of red material—these should be tied to wrists, heads, necks etc. Scarves marked City F.C.

City F.C.—this insignia can be printed by making a template and then stencilling on whatever is needed from coats to plastic refuse bags for clearing the pitch.

ACT I

The First Half at City Football ground. Afternoon

The moment prior to the kick-off of the afternoon league match between City F.C. and the psychopathic Bruddersford United

A busker is playing the "Match of the Day" theme in the C of the pitch as:

The crowd (audience) enter and take their places on the terrace

Off stage the City supporters can be heard revving up with cries of "programme" and "peanuts" etc.

A policeman enters and feels the busker's collar

The City F.C. groundstaff enter and applaud as:

The policeman exits with the busker as:

The supporters (off stage) and the crowd boo

A policewoman and some St John's ambulance personnel enter and filter onto the area as:

Loudspeaker (*reverb*) Good-afternoon ladies and gentlemen and welcome to the City Football Ground!

With a roar the supporters enter and pour onto the pitch by the different access points

The supporters, groundstaff, police, and the St John's personnel all clap and sing the opening number

All (*Clap-clap: clap-clap-clap: clap-clap-clap-clap*) City!
(*Clap-clap: clap-clap-clap: clap-clap-clap-clap*) City!
(*Clap-clap: clap-clap-clap: clap-clap-clap-clap*) City!

Song 1: City

All (*very loud and excited*)   City! City!
Isn't it a pity
You can't tell
Yer left foot from yer right!
Yer shootin's hit 'n miss
'Arf the time yer Brahms and Liszt
And you 'aven't scored a goal fer sixteen weeks!
City! City!
Where's yer nitty-gritty?

You must really try and give it some
Start dishin' out the dirties
Hack their shins and rip their shirties
Yes, just git us off
The bottom of the league.

But we'll support yer
And stick by yer
We will wear the red and white
Though the fullbacks are both toothless
And the midfield's bleedin' useless
They 'ave never let us down
So when Saturday comes round
We'll be out there in the crowd
Singin'
City
We luv you!

City! City!
Isn't it a pity
Isn't it a pity
We luv you!

The opening two verses only are repeated softly with same movements under the Loudspeaker's announcement

Music: 1a

Loudspeaker The team changes for this afternoon's match may differ from those printed in your official programme and are as follows ... Due to National Health and quarantine complications the place of I. Strain, City's injured goalkeeper, will be taken this afternoon by local favourite—Shaky Goggles!

Boos off stage by the City team

Only one change in the Bruddersford United side. The number five shirt will be worn by G.B.H. Hawkins—on weekend release. Now, here they come. It's the mean machine. It's City.

During the following the City team enter running

Supporters (*Clap-clap: clap-clap-clap: clap-clap-clap-clap*) City!
(*Clap-clap: clap-clap-clap: clap-clap-clap-clap*) City!
(*Clap-clap: clap-clap-clap: clap-clap-clap-clap*) City!

The City team are totally uncoordinated. They are gormless, inane and very funny

Shaky is led, complete with a white stick and dark glasses, to the goal and helped to feel the goal posts by Titch

Lofty takes huge captain-like bounds around the pitch, Enid practises pirouettes and pliés, while Tubs is totally unfit and out of breath

Act I 3

Titch runs to his place on the pitch, pulls up his shorts and completely blindfolds himself

Loudspeaker And a big hand please for today's visiting opponents. Those Yorkshire yobboes—Bruddersford United!
Supporters and crowd Booooo!

The City team take up their playing positions

Throughout the following the supporters, groundstaff etc. shout encouragement to the City team. "Show 'em your knickers, Enid!" and "Use your weight, Tubs!"

> *The Bruddersford team (all female) hurtle on. They are padded at the shoulders and biceps so that they resemble American Pro Footballers rather than English League Soccer players. They are aggressive in a humorous manner and intimidate not only the crowd but also the supporters*

The referee follows them giving a single blast on his whistle to accompany each step he takes

He places the ball on the centre spot. He blows his whistle for the start of the match. The two teams line up in playing positions. Einstein faces in the wrong direction. The referee blows his whistle for the kick-off. The players and the supporters move in slow motion. The Bruddersford mid-field player, Butcher, puts his foot on the ball as Butcher's team mates run in slow motion towards their City opposite numbers. In a series of funny choreographed and mimed punches and kicks they annihilate the City team who are left writhing in slow motion agony. During this sequence Butcher duffs up Lofty, and the Bruddersford's goalkeeper, I. Wrench moves the length of the pitch to do over Shaky. He busts his white stick, jumps on his dark glasses and pulls his polo-necked jumper over his head. While Shaky is blundering about, a second whistle blast by the referee signals a freeze. The Bruddersford and City players stay still until Butcher has the ball in front of the City goal

The Lights dim slightly

Butcher (*putting his foot on the ball*) Bruddersford's got t'ball.
Bruddersford team Bruddersford's got t'ball!
Butcher Bruddersford's goin' t'shoot. (*He takes his shooting foot back into position and freezes*)
Bruddersford team Bruddersford's goin' t'shoot!
Butcher Bruddersford's shot. (*He hits the ball into the back of the net*)
Bruddersford team Goal!

Everything moves back to normal speed as:

The Bruddersford team leap in the air. They mash in the referee and add a few more indiscriminate kicks to the injured City players

The supporters, encouraging the crowd to do the same, boo the Bruddersford side off the pitch

> *The Bruddersford players exit*

The St John's Ambulance rush on with stretchers to assist the stricken players and the referee. The stretcher material is only held in position by velcro strips which rip off when the players are lifted

The St John's Ambulance exit and run off carrying only the poles

The City players are cuddled, given babies' feeding bottles, wrapped in blankets etc.

The police, groundstaff and the City players exit as:

The supporters fill the area

Supporters (*singing*)   City! City!
Yer footwork's none too pretty
Runnin' round like kids
Wiv droopy drawers
Yer laces come undone
'Arf the time yer on yer bums
You'd be better off in ballet
That's a fact.
City! City!
Wot a load of titties (twitties)
'Arf of you are bandy and cross-eyed.
The skipper—wot a wally
He should star in "Hello Dolly"
'Cos 'e couldn't even burst a paper bag

But we'll support yer
And stick by yer
We will wear the red and white
Though our goalie
Is plain loco
And resembles Quasimodo
He has never let us down
So when Saturday comes round
We'll be out there in the crowd
Singin' "City we luv you".
City! City!
Isn't it a pity
Isn't it a pity
We
Luv
You!

(*Clap-clap: clap-clap-clap: clap-clap-clap clap*) City!

The supporters start to move off the area with the clapping fading away

(*Clap-clap: clap-clap-clap: clap-clap-clap-clap*) City! (*Clap-clap: clap-clap-clap: clap-clap-clap-clap*) City!

The supporters exit as:

Act I

The management of City F.C., Sheba, Benny, Sylv, Norbert and Daphne Vestal, each enter from a different corner of the pitch. They are fuming

Daphne carries a large pad and pencil

Sheba Pathetic!
Benny Useless!
Sylv Mentally deficient!
Norbert Certainly not one of their best games of the season.
Daphne I thought they tried quite hard really.
Sheba (*with a withering look*) Don't be stupid, Daphne!
Daphne Sorry.
Benny Thrashed. One-Nil.
Sylv In two minutes flat.
Benny Must be a world record for incompetence.
Sheba It's certainly a world record for cowardice. Not one win in sixteen weeks.
Norbert That is bad I admit.
Sheba Bad! Norbert, that team of sub-intelligent cripples couldn't beat an old people's home!
Benny They've been party to one of football's greatest fiascos this afternoon.
Sheba I think we have no alternative but to call an emergency——

Two groundstaff enter, with a table

Two groundstaff (*plonking down a table* CS) Board meeting!

The groundstaff exit

Sheba Right, so please draw up your——

Four groundstaff enter, with four chairs

Four groundstaff (*plonking down the four chairs round the table*) Chairs.

The groundstaff exit

Sheba Right, and let us review the situation. (*She sits*)

Benny, Sylv and Norbert sit

Daphne (*scribbling*) Review the s-i-t-u-a-t-i-o-n.

Benny starts to suck his thumb

Sheba As chairwoman of the City Football Club I must point out— Benjamin!

They all look at Benny

Thumb!
Benny (*removing his thumb noisily*) Sorry dear.
Sheba I must point out that quite frankly the organisation at management level is diabolical.
Benny Useless.

Sylv Mentally deficient.
Norbert Certainly not out of the top drawer.
Sheba And only one person can be held responsible.

They all look at Benny

Benny Quite. (*He begins to pick his nose*)
Norbert Well, I feel partly responsible.
Sheba (*touching his hand affectionately*) No Norbert, I don't hold you responsible in any way. I know as coach that you do your very best—Benjamin!

The all look at Benny

Finger!
Benny Sorry dear. (*He removes his finger*)
Sheba The plain facts of the matter are that the Club does appear to be all at sea.
Sylv Riding on the crest of a slump.
Sheba Don't be a plonker, Sylvia.
Sylv (*mimicking Benny*) Sorry, dear.
Daphne Shall I make notes of everything you say, Mrs Shekelstein?
Sheba Only of those points which are particular to Club business, Daphne. We don't want a best selling novel.
Benny Those pads and pencils cost money, already.
Sheba *My* money, Benjamin.
Benny Of course, beloved.
Sylv (*painting her nails*) Haven't we got off the point?
Norbert What point?
Sylv The point that City Football Club is falling to pieces.
Norbert I thought that your mother had made that point quite clear.
Sheba (*gently*) Thank you Norbert. (*Snapping*) And may I remind you, madam, that we won't put those pieces together again if you spend half your time sitting about daubing your nails with Dulux emulsion.
Benny Making eyes at all and sundry.
Sylv Who?
Benny You, chatting up the tea-boy—of all people.
Sylv Well, he's nice.
Sheba Nice. Nice. Tea-boys—nice. You have no chic, Sylvia. I can't imagine where this vulgarity stems from.
Norbert I wouldn't mind a nice cup of tea.
Sheba Of course, Norbert—an excellent idea. Daphne!
Daphne Yes, Mrs Shekelstein?
Sheba Where is the tea-boy?
Daphne Oh yeah, I nearly forgot, he left this little love letter for you, Sylvia. (*She goes to pass Sylv a crumpled piece of what looks suspiciously like toilet paper*)
Sylv A love letter? (*She takes the piece of paper*)
Sheba (*snatching it out of Sylv's hand*) A love letter? Is this it?
Daphne Yeah, he was in a hurry.

Act I

Sheba Obviously. (*She unravels the paper and puts on her glasses; reading*)
> "Roses are red
> Violets are blue
> Gone for a pint
> Be back at two"

Charming!
Daphne (*dreamily*) It's lovely.
Sheba (*ignoring Daphne's stupidity*) So this is the best that your man of the moment can conjure up, is it Sylvia?
Benny Some lines stolen from the immortal Shakestein and scribbled on Club stationery.
Sylv It's a joke.
Benny A joke?
Sylv Yeah, Joe likes making jokes. Anyway, we weren't discussing him. I thought we were discussing ways of improving the team.
Daphne You need some new talent.
Benny We could do with some new blood in the side.
Norbert We could do with a nice cup of tea—but we ain't goin' to get it.
Sheba (*secreting the note and moving behind Benny's chair*) New players would involve expense, Benjamin.
Benny Well, let's develop expensive tastes.
Norbert Like biscuits.
Sylv What's our financial situation?
Sheba Fluid.
Sylv Meaning?
Daphne We're going down the drain. (*She laughs*)

There is silence

Sorry.
Sheba (*through clenched teeth*) Do you want to lose that pad and pencil, Daphne?
Daphne No, Mrs Shekelstein.
Sheba Good, then kindly keep your little pearls of distorted wisdom to yourself.
Daphne Yes, Mrs Shekelstein.
Sheba We are not in any kind of financial difficulty.
Norbert Great.
Sheba The City F.C. has always been fortunate enough to be able to draw from the generous estate left to Benjamin by my late lamented father on the day of our marriage——
Benny Rest in peace, Isaac—wherever you're negotiating.
Sheba —and it can continue to rely on such support for as long as the Shekelstein Corset and Swimwear Empire keeps its head above water.
Norbert You're wonderful, Mrs S.
Sheba Of course, Norbert.
Benny (*breaking the mood*) Well, if we've got the mazooma, why don't we splash out and buy a couple of new players?

Sheba Because we don't make rash, hasty decisions, that's why.
Norbert You know, it might not be a question of *new* players but more a question of *new* training methods and skills.
Sylv Well, Norby, you're the coach. How do you rate their skills?
Norbert Well, their main weakness is the physical inability to cope with para-linear and spheroid control in any dynamic confrontation.
Sylv Meaning?
Norbert They're crap.
Benny Exactly.
Norbert Mind you, we had a weak side in eighty-eight and I managed to pull them into shape.
Benny The glorious past, already.
Sheba We must look to the future, Norbert, you know what happens if you just rest on our laurels.
Daphne You get squashed laurels.
Sheba (*livid*) That's it!

Sheba snatches Daphne's pad and pencil away

Daphne (*screaming*) Aaaiiieeeooouuu!
Sheba (*thinking that Daphne is hysterical*) All right Daphne. Calm Down. Don't get hysterical.

Sheba hands Daphne the pad and pencil

Here. See you're reinstated.
Daphne No, it's not that, Mrs Shekelstein. It's Miss Sylvia. (*She points at Sylv*)

They all jump out of their seats or step back and stare at Sylv

Benny What about her?
Daphne It's her wossaname!
Benny Wossaname?
Daphne Her thingy.
Sheba Thingy?
Daphne Her T-Shirt.
Norbert What about her T-Shirt?
Daphne Somefink moved underneath it.
Sheba Moved?
Daphne Yeah—wriggled.

They all stare at Sylv's T-shirt and something does appear to move

All (*apart from Sylv*) Aaaiiieeeooouuu.
Daphne There it goes again.
Benny Oh my gawd!
Sylv It's all right Daphne—it's only Gazza.

There is a pause

Sheba Pardon?
Sylv I said it's only Gazza.

Act I

Sheba And what, in the name of all that's Golders Green, is Gazza!
Sylv My 'amster.
Sheba Your 'amster!
Norbert Livin' in your T-shirt?
Sylv Why not—sometimes I keep 'im in me handbag.
Sheba A handbag! (*She realises what's she's said!*)
Benny First a tea-boy—now a hamster.
Sheba When, Sylvia, are you going to cease befriending these orphaned creatures?
Sylv I like lookin' after 'em.
Daphne She's got a hedgehog behind her bookcase.
Benny Her room's like a blinkin' safari park.
Sheba Benjamin—don't be vulgar. Sylvia—get rid of it. It's quite disgusting.
Sylv I love him.
Benny I wish you could show the same enthusiasm about the fate of our Club as you do about rodents.
Daphne She's got a rat in her wardrobe.
Benny Shut up!
Sheba Benjamin is for once talking like a human being.
Benny Thank you, dear.
Sheba Enthusiasm is what we need.
Norbert Ambition.
Benny A plan.
Sylv For the future.
Sheba To ensure success once again in the first division.
Daphne She's got a snake an' all.
All (*apart from Daphne*) Shut up!

They form a group around Sheba who stands on the table

The whole number should be done as a "cod" Gilbert and Sullivan. The gestures and the choreography should be reminiscent of D'Oyle Carte. You may have a grand finale where the chorus gets larger and larger until in the end the area is filled with supporters, groundstaff, police, St John's Ambulance etc.

Song 2: She's Gorn and Thrown a Wobbly

Sheba	Our objectives now are clear
	We must face the facts austere
	There's no place for sobs or tears
	Or sucking thumbs (*looking at Benny*) or stupid sneers (*looking at Daphne*)
All	The team we have is hopeless
	It is lazy, gross and dim
	So we must start to get it
	Fighting fit and looking trim.
Sheba	Just give me your attention and I'll tell you what I'll do
	I'll train all those malingerers until they're black and blue

All	She'll train all those malingerers until they're black and blue.
Sheba	Each little fault or foible and each drib-bi-ling defect In those stupid senseless puddings I'll endeavour to correct.
All	In those stupid senseless puddings she'll endeavour to correct.
Sheba	To all their little weaknesses a lever I will prise And little plans to catch them out I'll certainly devise
All	And little plans to catch them out she'll certainly devise
Sheba	I want to see them training till their muscles are all sore And any player skiving I will nail into the floor.
All	And any player skiving she will nail into the floor. Oh my gawd She's gorn and lost her marbles, Marbles, marbles, She's goin' round the twist Stone me rigid She's gorn and thrown a wobbly Wobbly, wobbly, She's gorn and flipped her lid!
Sheba	I'm certainly no lady, I'm as pleasant as a slap And I'll strangle any shirker with his unwashed jockey-strap.
All	Yes, she'll strangle any shirker with his unwashed jockey-strap.
Sheba	Real talent and ambition that is what I'm striking for And players who will give me more and more and more and more
All	Those players who will give her more and more and more and more.
Sheba	I love my fellow creatures but I'll tell you in all truth I can't stand fairy poofters, gnomes or strange exotic fruits.
All	She can't stand fairy poofters, gnomes or strange exotic fruits.
Sheba	So any City player, friends, who does not bend his knee Will taste the shining sharpness of my little snicker snee.
All	Will taste the shining sharpness of her little snicker snee. Oh my gawd She's gone and lost her marbles Marbles, marbles She's going round the twist Stone me rigid She's gorn and thrown a wobbly Wobbly, wobbly She's gorn and done her crust She's gorn and done She's gorn and done She has really gorn and done Her crust!

Joe Rabbit enters at the end of the number pushing a tea-trolley at breakneck speed. He screeches to a halt

Joe (*addressing the management*) One lump or two?
Sheba You are late.
Joe Yeah, sorry about that. I got caught in the rough-hour traffic!
Sheba The bookies more like.
Benny (*feeling the urn*) The tea's cold.
Norbert There's no biscuits.
Joe Only one (*He gives it to Daphne*)
Daphne (*to the audience*) He's nice. I like him.
Sylv (*sexily*) Hallo—Joe.

They all freeze, apart from Sylv, and look at Joe

Joe (*sexily*) Hallo—Sylv.

They all freeze, apart from Joe, and look at Sylv

Sylv I think you're great.

They all look at Joe

Joe Me too.

They all look at Sheba, apart from Joe and Sylv

Sheba Any other compliments, Mr——?
Joe Rabbit, Joe Rabbit.
Sheba Rabbit?
Joe Yeah, as in bunny girl.
Sheba So, why are you late?
Joe Ah well, I was busy making something especially for you, Mrs Shekelstein—a nice cup of Rosie Lee. (*He holds out a cup to her stirring vigorously*)

Sheba takes the cup, sweeps past Joe and dumps it on the table

Sheba No, thank you!
Joe Sorry about that.

Benny puts his finger in Sheba's abandoned cup

Sheba Benjamin!

They all look at Benjamin

   Finger!
Benny (*extracting his finger and sucking it*) Sorry, dear.
Joe He can 'ave it if he likes.
Sheba He doesn't want it.
Joe Pardon me for living.
Norbert (*running on the spot although he's not very fit*) Well, Mrs S., your plan's inspired me. I'll get the lads training first thing tomorrow morning.
Sheba Good. I shall also employ some of my dancing school exercises on them. Tone up—hidden muscles.
Joe Sounds nasty.

Norbert (*out of breath*) We'll transform the entire team in less than six weeks.

Benny scratches his bum

Sheba Excellent. Norbert—bring the table. Daphne—cup. Benjamin!

They all look at Benny

　Fingers!

Benjamin stops as:

　Daphne and Norbert exit
　Benjamin.
Benny Yes, dear?
Sheba The chairs.
Benny Yes, dear.

Benny exits, struggling with all four chairs

Joe is about to put his arms round Sylv

Sheba Rabbit!
Joe Yes, dear?
Sheba Keep your mucky paws off my daughter!
Joe (*whipping his hands away*) Yes, dear.

Sheba exits

　(*Looking after Sheba in disbelief*) Blimey, she should have been in the paratroopers.
Sylv She was.
Joe Eh?!
Sylv Well she's always been bossy, been like it for years and years.
Joe How old is she then?
Sylv 'Bout fifty-three comin' on death.
Joe Have the National Trust heard about her?
Sylv She's probably got shares in it. She thinks she owns everybody.
Joe Where did all her money come from then?
Sylv (*"cod" American*) The Shekelstein Empire!
Joe What? A cinema?
Sylv No, her father, Isaac Shekelstein.
Joe You've lost me.
Sylv Shekelsteins—the biggest manufacturers of underwear in the U.K.
Joe Blimey—so you mean to say that her and old Benny have had a hand in nearly every bra in Great Britain?
Sylv Figuratively speaking—yes.
Joe (*interested*) So—you're loaded then?
Sylv You could say that.
Joe I just did. (*He puts an arm round her, then retracts it quickly*) Blimey, Sylv, you got fleas?
Sylv Do you mind.

Act I

Joe Well, sunnink just moved.
Sylv Moved?
Joe Yeah, wriggled under your wossaname.
Sylv Oh don't you start. It's only Gazza havin' a scratch.
Joe Oh no, it's not that blinkin' hamster again, is it?
Sylv I can't help it.
Joe You could try.
Sylv I like hamsters—anyway he's a pedigree.
Joe I like hot dogs, Sylv, but I don't 'ave 'em registered at the Kennel Club.
Sylv Does it put you off, then?
Joe Put me off? Bleedin' Norah, Sylv—it is a bit disturbing to slip your arm round your bird to find that the most attractive parts of her anatomy keep movin'about.
Sylv Could be interestin'.
Joe Leave it out. Suppose we was married?
Sylv What d'you mean?
Joe Well it wouldn't be very romantic would it?
Sylv Romantic?
Joe Well imagine, (*he cuddles up close to Sylv*) early evening, we've just snuggled down together in bed.
Sylv Yeah.
Joe I've turned to you.
Sylv (*getting carried away*) Yeah.
Joe I've taken you in my arms.
Sylv Yeah!
Joe Only to ...
Sylv Only to what, Joe?
Joe Only to spot a bleedin' hamster disappearing down yer nightie!
Sylv Don't exaggerate.
Joe Exaggerate—blimey! It'd be like kippin' down in London Zoo every night.
Sylv I'd only keep Gazza.
Joe That is a really romantic incentive, Sylv.
Sylv Who said I'd marry you anyway?
Joe There's no one else is there?
Sylv There must be—somewhere.
Joe Knock it off. I might not be much of a catch at the moment, Sylv, but one day you might want to change that hamster for a Rabbit.

Sylvia giggles

It wasn't that funny, Sylv.
Sylv No, it was Gazza!
Joe What?
Sylv He just wiped his nose on one of me wobblies.
Joe (*shouting at Gazza inside Sylv's T-shirt*) Shove off!
Sylv You're jealous.
Joe (*shouting at Gazza*) No I'm not.
Sylv Yes you are.

Joe No I'm not. I just get riled cos' yer mother thinks I'm useless, you think I'm useless and I think—I'm useless.

The music starts for song 3

Joe lifts Sylv gently up on to the tea-trolley which can be used in the choreography and business for the duet

Song 3: A Little Bit of Me

(*Singing*)
Don't think that I'm a wally
Cos I push this blinkin' trolley
Shoutin' "one lump or two"
Don't take me for a nutter
Cos I sometimes 'ave a flutter
And lose a quid or two.
You know I idolise yer, Sylv
I've always idolised yer, Sylv
And it's time I made it clear
That
Some blokes 'ave got it
And I've got a lot of it
I've got a lot of what it takes
And if you want a bit of it
Just a little bit
Don't muck about
Just say that
You'd like a little bit
Just a little bit
You'd like a little bit of me.

Sylv
Don't think that I'm a teaser
Cos I don't do things to please yer
Whisperin' "I love you"
Cos you know I tend to burble
'Bout furry things like gerbils
'Stead of talkin' to you
You know I idolise yer, Joe
I've always idolised yer, Joe
And it's time I made it clear
That
Some birds 'ave got it
And I've got a lot of it
I've got a lot of what it takes
And if you want a bit of it
Just a little bit of it
Don't muck about
Just say that
You'd like a little bit
Just a little bit
You'd like a little bit of me.

Act I

Joe and **Sylv** So
Both of us have got it
And we've got a lot of it
We've got a lot of what it takes
And if we want a bit of it
Just a little bit of it

Joe picks up a bottle of washing-up liquid

We won't muck about
Just say that
We'd like a little bit
Just a little bit of it
We'd like a little bit of us!

As Joe and Sylv move together for a kiss, the bottle of washing-up liquid Joe's holding is squashed and a great fountain of water squirts upwards and down on them

The Lights fade to Black-out and then come up brightly

A cock crows

Joe 'Ere, Sylv.
Sylv What?
Joe It's mornin' already.
Sylv Blimey that was quick.
Joe Yeah, well, I don't 'ang about.

Off stage we can hear the voices of the City team and Norbert's whistle

It's the City lads. They've started training already. What's the time?
Sylv (*calling into the wings*) What's the time?
Offstage voice Six o'clock!
Sylv (*to Joe*) It's six o'clock.
Joe Six o'clock—blimey they are gettin' keen.
Sylv Come on Joe, I'll cook you something special for breakfast.
Joe Gerbilburgers?
Sylv No!—how about sausage, egg and chips?
Joe Wiv toast?
Sylv You're on.
Joe Lovely!

Joe and Sylv exit, running as:

We hear the whistle and Norbert enters running, carrying the ball. He is in his City tracksuit and flat cap. He bounces the ball vigorously but it either flies off at a tangent or bounces up and hits Norbert in the privates. Either way—he looks pathetic

Norbert (*out of breath*) Come on lads. Move it!

The City team, Lofty, Titch, Tubs, Einstein, Enid and Shaky run in—if you can call it running. When they eventually line up—they pant as if they've just completed a marathon

Norbert Right. Lovely. Poetry in motion.

The team make noises of approval, "Thanks Norbert" etc.

How d'you feel lads?
Lofty Magic.
Enid I think I've reached my pinnacle.
Titch And he don't often do that, Norbert.
Tubs When's breakfast?
Einstein My—brain—is—in—a—whirl.
Shaky I'm completely far—far—far—fagged out.
Norbert OK lads settle down and listen carefully. Today we start a new schedule.

When they hear the word "schedule" it stops them in their tracks and they freeze. They are concerned—as it sounds like hard work

Lofty (*suspiciously*) A new schedule of what?
Norbert A new schedule of training.
Team Aaaaaagghh! (*They all scream and either faint on the spot or go to run off the area*)
Norbert Get back 'ere.

The team return slowly and apprehensively

Lofty, you are the skipper of the City side and as such you should be setting an example to the rest of the younger players.

The team look behind them searching for these so-called 'younger' players

Lofty Point taken, Norbert. It's just that we're very nervous of technical words like—(*he daren't say it*) like—schedule.

The team whimper and rush round Lofty clutching onto his arms, legs and clothing in fear

All right lads (*He cuddles them in*) Steady. Trust Lofty.
Titch (*to Norbert*) You shouldn't spring things like that on us suddenly.
Enid Brusquely.
Titch Yes, brusquely. That's a very good description, Enid.
Einstein Bully.
Tubs When's breakfast?
Shaky Made me all, far—far—far—nervous.
Norbert Well there's nothing to be nervous about lads. It's simply a policy of altering the 'style' of things. (*He's done it again—a new suspicious word*)

The team freeze again and cringe

Shaky (*stuttering*) New stir—stir—stir—style of what?
Norbert New style of exercise.
Team (*screaming; fainting*) Aaaaaghggh!
Norbert Look, stop friggin' about. This is serious. The City chairwoman——
Tubs Mrs Shekelstein?

Norbert Yes, the lady that pays your wages each week has decided, after watching your pathetic display against Bruddersford, that the missing factor in our play is teamwork.
Titch Teamwork?
Norbert Yes, playing with each other.
Enid Now that sounds more like it.
Norbert Now as you may know, Sheba——
Team Aye aye! (*There is a great deal of nudging and winking as if to suggest that Norbert is getting 'plenty of something'*) Sheba! Naughty Norbert!
Norbert (*speaking over the top of them*) As you may know, Mrs Shekelstein runs a top class dancing academy in the city and she reckons that by employing the same kind of techniques used in dancing she can improve our game.
Titch Dancin's for fairies.
Tubs Well you're a sort of gnome Titch—that should be right up your toadstool.
Enid Well, I rather like the sound of the idea.
Titch You would.
Shaky Do you think this dancin' might help to car—car—car—calm my nerves, Lofty?
Lofty Could be the very thing, Shaky.
Norbert Look, this isn't the Citizens Advice Bureau—so stop all the whittering. Mrs S. has laid down all the basic griff on an instructional tape.
Tubs When's the boss comin', Norbert?
Norbert She's comin' in a couple of minutes to 'ave a dekko at our progress. So we'd better get in some practice. Einstein!
Einstein Yes—Norb?
Norbert Wheel on the tape recorder.
Einstein (*speaking slowly*) Wheel—on—the—tape—recorder.

Einstein exits and returns with a trolley with a tape recorder on it

Norbert The rest of you find a working space.

Einstein twiddles with the knobs on the tape recorder

Titch Einstein's poncin' about with the knobs, Norbert.
Norbert Einstein, stop poncin' about with the knobs and come over here.
Einstein Right.
Norbert Lofty turn it on and *all* of you pay attention and follow the instructions.
Lofty Tape on, Norb.

A chime should sound at each of the following asterisks

Taped voice (*female, soft and sultry; from the recorder*) *Football for beginners. Lesson One. *"Facing the facts." Repeat after me, "We are useless."
Team (*shouting at the top of their voices*) We are useless!
Taped voice No need to shout.

Team (*whispering*) We are useless.
Taped voice Better.
Team (*whispering*) Thank you.
Taped voice You're welcome. Football for beginners. Lesson two *"Breathing." Ready? Breathe in.
Team (*speaking the words*) Breathe in.
Taped voice (*slightly irritated*) No, you don't say breathe in. You actually do breathe in.
Team Oh?
Taped voice Lesson Three *"Football skills through dance." Ready?
Team Yes.
Taped voice Good, this is your secret weapon. This is the way to win. With me. Begin.

The team follow the instructions and movements making appropriate noises at the end of sentences

There is no music at this point

Taped voice (*unmusical and mechanical*) You put your left boot in.
Team Oooo!

Einstein puts his right foot forward, the team draw his attention to the error and he corrects it

Taped voice You put your left boot out.
Team Aah!
Taped voice In—out, in—out.
  You boot 'em all about.
Team Yeah!
Taped voice You do the cobbler crunching
Team Oof!
Taped voice And you nut 'em quick.
Team Splat!
Taped voice Cos that's what it's all about.

The team have obviously enjoyed the above

Taped voice Now—do you think you can do that all together?
Team (*shouting enthusiastically*) Yes!
Taped voice Good. Then this time with the music.

Song 3a: Hokey Cokey

The team now dances the number in the style of the "hokey cokey" but adding the chorus at the end

Team   You put your left boot in
             Your left boot out
             In—out, in—out
             You boot 'em all about
             You do the cobbler crunching
             And you nut 'em quick

Act I

>Cos that's what it's all about
>Oh the shattered shinbones
>Oh the knackered kneecaps
>Oh the punctured pillocks
>Knees up, stamp hard.
>Kick 'em off the park!

Norbert Well what d'you think, lads?
Team Great Norb!
Lofty It's great to have a plan at last, Einstein what's your watch say?

Einstein puts his watch to his eye

Voice off stage Half past eight!
Einstein (*to Lofty*) Quarter to nine.
Lofty Half past eight! Mrs S. should be coming.
Shaky She is coming. She's coming ri—ri—ri——

Sheba and Benny sweep in, both in tracksuits

Sheba *Right* now.
Lofty Smarten yourselves up, lads. In line.

The team line up in front of the goal

Sheba inspects them quickly from Titch at one end to Lofty at the other

Sheba My God! I've never seen such a flea-bag ridden shower.
Lofty (*annoyed*) 'Ere, 'old on a minute.
Sheba Who are you?
Lofty Head flea.
Benny That I can believe.
Norbert (*stepping in*) The lads have worked very hard on the instructional tape.
Titch We're exhausted.
Sheba (*towering over him*) You don' look very exhausted to me.
Benny May I remind you that there's always been a tradition in this club that every player will train until he drops.
Tubs I never heard that before.
Benny Course you haven't. (*He points at Tubs*) The tradition didn't start until six o'clock this morning.
Sheba Benjamin!

They all look at Benjamin

   Finger!
Benny (*stopping pointing*) Sorry, heart throb.
Sheba Nobody asked for your opinion.
Benny (*downtrodden*) Course not.
Sheba Kindly remember that you are only the manager of this club and therefore have absolutely nothing to do with decision making.
Benny Nothing at all, passion fruit.
Sheba (*soft and sexy*) Norbert.

Team (*echoing her word and manner*) Norbert.
Sheba (*looking at them reprovingly*) Norbert, I am pleased that they have mastered the dance tape. It's a pity that they resemble over-weight gorillas.
Tubs There's no need to be personal.
Norbert Belt up, Tubs.
Benny Stop showing off.
Sheba And start fighting the flab!

Song 4: The Muscle-Hustle

This song should be sung and danced as a rock'n'roll number

Sheba, Benny and **Norbert**
Now once you've got the rhythm
And you're feeling fine
You want to lose some ounzes
For the very first time
Swing like Elvis Presley
Keep those hips in line
Then do the muscle-hustle
And you're fine, fine, fine.

Team
Do the muscle-hustle
Grunt and groan.
Do the muscle-hustle
Grunt and groan
Do the muscle-hustle
Grunt and groan
Do the muscle-hustle
And you're fine, fine, fine, fine.
Stretch those arms
Snap 'em tight
Let's swing 'em around
Bounce those hips
Left and right
Let's sweat off a pound
Bend those knees
Shoot those legs
Let's roll it around
And do the muscle-hustle
All over town.

Sheba, Benny and **Norbert**
Now when you've had a breather
And it's time to refresh
Remember ice-cold lager
Means a bulge in the vest
Swing like Elvis Presley
Keep those hips in line
And do the hippo-hopper
Just one more time.

Team
Do the hippo-hopper

	Shake it out
	Do the hippo-hopper
	Shake it out
	Do the hippo-hopper
	Shake it out
	Do the hippo-hopper
	Just one more time.
	Stretch those arms
	Snap 'em tight
	Let's swing 'em around
	Bounce those hips
	Left and right
	Let's sweat off a pound
	Bend those knees
	Shoot those legs
	Let's hold it around
	And do the hippo-hopper
	All over town.
Sheba, Benny and **Norbert**	Now if you've lost your muscles
	And they've all gone to seed
	Your tummy's like a dumpling
	Hanging down to your knees
	Swing like Elvis Presley
	Keep those hips in line
	And do the jumbo-jiver
	Just one more time
Team	Do the jumbo-jiver
	Twist and shout
	Do the jumbo-jiver
	Twist and shout
	Do the jumbo-jiver
	Twist and shout
	Do the jumbo-jiver
	And you're fine fine
	Fine!

The team collapse

Norbert Blimey, they're shattered!
Sheba As they should be.
Lofty (*feeling parts of his body*) I've gone numb—all over.
Shaky I'm completely far—far—far—knackered.
Titch I've shrunk.
Tubs Impossible.
Einstein I fink I've got brain damage.
Tubs Even more impossible.
Enid Well, I feel like a new man.
Tubs Now that is possible!
Benny Attention please, lads.

Sheba stands agog at the audacity of Benny taking control

    Now remember that it's the return match against Bruddersford United on Wednesday, in the quarter finals of the World six-a-side Cup Championship. You must be fighting fit and concentrating on victory. OK?
Team OK.
Benny Now, off to the showers.

The team all start to run off

Sheba Stop!

The team freeze in their tracks

    Stay!

The team lift their arms up like dogs' paws

    Sit!

The team kneel, paws still up

    Since when have you been giving instructions in this club?
Benny Sorry, treasure heart. (*He goes down like the players*)
Sheba I should think so. Now remember that it's the return match against Bruddersford United on Wednesday, in the quarter finals of the World six-a-side Cup Championship. You must be fighting fit and concentrating on victory. Now—off to the showers.

The team run off, making doggie noises

    Benjamin.
Benny Yes dear?
Sheba Sweatband. (*She removes the sweatband from her brow for Benny to carry*)
Benny Of course, my little temptress. (*He starts to exit but overhears Sheba's next line*)
Sheba Norbert—(*silkily and sensuously*) I would like to see you in my office later this evening for private conference and—team tactics.
Norbert Of course—Sheebikins.

Norbert, Sheba and Benny exit from different access points

The arena is empty for a moment until:

The two changing-room ladies—Mrs Rinse and Mrs Brillo enter. They wear wrap-over aprons and headscarves and carry City F.C. refuse bags

Music 4a: Entrance of Mrs Brillo and Mrs Rinse

Six shower girls enter from another entrance carrying six chairs. They wear shower caps and place towels on the backs of the chairs which are placed alternately on arena stage and all facing out on end stage. The shower girls also have little watering-cans painted in City colours holding warm water

Act I

Mrs Rinse and Mrs Brillo have a towel each and go to one entrance area and call out. They both love men and sport in that order but have got faces like punctured footballs

Mrs Brillo (*shouting off*) Showers are ready, lads!

The team respond off stage

Mrs Rinse (*excitedly*) And you'll have to take all your clothes off.
Mrs Brillo The water's lovely and warm.

The team respond off stage

Mrs Rinse But you'll have to take all your clothes off.

Mrs Rinse and Mrs Brillo are nearly beside themselves in anticipation

Mrs Brillo And remember to dry yourselves properly.

The team respond off stage

Mrs Rinse (*building up to it*) When—you've taken all your clothes off!
Mrs Brillo (*noticing that Mrs Rinse is going to get over-excited*) All right, Edna. Steady. Better take one of your thingies.
Mrs Rinse Probably best. (*She stuffs a handful of tablets down from her shaking hand*)
Mrs Brillo In you come. Showers are ready!

The team suddenly burst in. They have removed their track shoes but are still wearing their socks. They are very noisy as they enter, very excited etc. Ad-lib dialogue as they run to their respective showers/chairs

The strip-streaker-flasher ballet

Music 4b: Strip Streak Flasher

The whole sequence must be choreographed like a 'strip' to the music

The six showergirls are frozen in position. One arm bent upwards representing a lever which when pulled downwards will tip up the watering-can held upright in the other hand. The strip sequence below refers to the garment to be removed and the action taken related to that garment. Each action must be completed in four beats of the music. The symbol "4" is given to show the time allowed to complete the movement. This will need careful rehearsal and should be very funny. Each character strips in character e.g. Lofty—bold, Enid—sexy. Shaky—fumbles, Einstein—confused, Tubs—struggles and Titch—shy

The music starts

Each character wears below his track suit bottoms—a pair of white shorts and below the white shorts a pair of swimming trunks or briefs on which are written the words 'City supporters'

Mrs Brillo and Mrs Rinse collect some of the cast-offs, before moving to the side to watch, mesmerised

Track suit top sequence
1. Unzip track suit top (4)
2. Remove left arm (4)
3. Remove right arm (4)
4. Swing top round and then throw (4)

Track suit bottoms sequence
5. Pull down bottoms shyly (4)
6. Pull back up hurriedly (4)
7. Pull down again boldly (4)
8. Remove and kick away (4)

Sock sequence
9. Sit down on the chair (4)
10. Remove left sock (4)
11. Swing and throw sock (4)
12. Remove right sock (4)
13. Swing sock and throw (4)
14. Wiggle toes (4)

Shower sequence
15. Stand and pull Shower girl's handle (4)
16. Rub sprinkling water all over face and body—make noises (8)
17. Pick up towel (4)
18. Adjust towel for rubbing back (4)
19. Rub back from towel over right shoulder and down to left hip (4)
20. Rub back in the opposite direction (4)
21. Adjust towel so it is held behind botty (4)
22. Rub botty (4)

Short removing sequence
23. Pull towel round body (4)
24. Fold it round and tuck in firmly (8)
25. Hands up under towel (4)
26. Pull down shorts to floor (4)
27. Kick shorts away (4)
28. Run towards the audience (4)
29. Stop and stand still, hands ready at tucked in section of towel (4)
30. Whip towels open and flash 'City supporters' briefs.*

*In the original production the players had huge saveloys tied round their waists—and at the end of The Strip, whipped them off and ate them as they exited. All a question of bravery really.

Lofty, Einstein, Tubs and Titch scream and then exit, running

Enid who is now thoroughly caught up in the whole thing and parades towards Mrs Brillo and Mrs Rinse as the music continues. The music stops abruptly as he halts in front of them. He gives a grand flash and opens his towel. He stands there for a moment in all his glory

Mrs Rinse and Mrs Brillo peer forward at his briefs and look at each other

Mrs Brillo Poor little sod/devil.

Act I

Enid exits totally depressed and sadly dragging his towel behind him

Mrs Rinse Aaah I feel really sorry for him.
Mrs Brillo Yes the spirit was willing but the flesh was weak.

Mrs Brillo and Mrs Rinse laugh

Mrs Rinse 'Ere, come on Edna. Let's start getting this changing room cleaned up.
Mrs Brillo Right.

The shower girls exit. They take four chairs, the watering-cans and any odd clothing near at hand

Mrs Brillo and Mrs Rinse clear up the residue of clothing in plastic bags marked City F.C. refuse

Mrs Rinse (*stopping work*) Hildegard!
Mrs Brillo Yes, Edna?
Mrs Rinse Did you notice the look Mrs S gave Norbert just before they left?
Mrs Brillo I certainly did.
Mrs Rinse Do you reckon she fancies 'im?
Mrs Brillo Course she does.
Mrs Rinse I feel sorry for her husband.
Mrs Brillo What Benny?
Mrs Rinse Yeah poor old devil. He daren't open his mouth.
Mrs Brillo Well, Edna—(*moving closer*) I can tell you something that not many people know.
Mrs Rinse What's that, Hildegard?
Mrs Brillo Well—I never like to repeat gossip.
Mrs Rinse Course not.
Mrs Brillo So listen very carefully the first time.
Mrs Rinse Right.
Mrs Brillo Old Benny's her tenth.
Mrs Rinse What, husband?
Mrs Brillo (*nodding*) Mind you, they do say that she liked the last one so much—she kept 'im on for an extra fortnight.
Mrs Rinse Get away.
Mrs Brillo As City is my only club—it's the truth, Edna.
Mrs Rinse The two-faced old tea-bag.
Mrs Brillo Never trust her, Edna. She's the kind of woman that puts her arm round your shoulder in front of your face——
Mrs Rinse Then smacks you in the mouth behind your back.
Mrs Brillo Exactly, Edna.
Mrs Rinse 'Ere we aren't gettin' on very fast are we? They're playin' those Bruddersford brutes again on Wednesday night in the cup game.
Mrs Brillo That'll be another massacre.
Mrs Rinse Mind you—this is the part of the day that can go as slow as it likes for me.
Mrs Brillo How d'you mean, dear?
Mrs Rinse You know sortin' out all the lads' dirty football kit. I love it.

Mrs Brillo Feels all warm and manly you mean?
Mrs Rinse Yeah, sometimes I get quite carried away (*She is!*)
Mrs Brillo I should 'ave another one of your doodahs if I was you.

Mrs Rinse bungs a few more pills down herself

Mrs Rinse (*trance like*) Gently rinsing Lofty's socks.
Mrs Brillo (*trance like*) Sewin' up the splits in Tubs's shorts.
Mrs Rinse Shortenin' the legs on Titch's underpants.
Mrs Brillo I wouldn't swap my job for a whole fortnight in Hollywood with that Tom Crude.
Mrs Rinse Well, I wouldn't say no to a bit of that, Hildegard.
Mrs Brillo I would. They can have all them filth stars.

Song 5: Sortin' out the Socks on Saturday

(*Singing*)
Some women like to live it up
And trip the light fantastic
Or play at dice and chat up blokes
In night clubs, orgiastic.
Some spend a fortune on fast cars
All glitter gaudiastic
But I like washin' filthy shorts
And scrubbin' socks elastic!

Mrs Rinse and Mrs Brillo
We like
Sortin' out the socks on Saturday
Soakin' all the shorts in suds
Cos sortin' out the socks on Saturday
Is the nearest thing to love
We get teeny tiny shivers
And erotic little quivers
When we slide our hands inside
Cos nothin' is more sexy
Than a sock all soft and flexy
That's been sorted out on Saturday by us.

Mrs Rinse
Some women dream of paradise
With sandy shores to lie on
Like Tenerife or Felixstowe
And champers to get high on
Some others chase big hunky blokes
With hairy chests to sigh on
But Hild' and me like washing pants
And scrubbing shorts
Bri-nylon!

Mrs Brillo and Mrs Rinse
We like sortin' out the socks on Saturday
Soakin' all the stuff in suds
Cos sortin' out the socks on Saturday
Is the nearest thing to love

Act I

> When we wash their smalls tomorrah
> It's like sodom and gomorrah
> All those ankles, legs and thighs
> And we give a little wink
> As we squeeze them in the sink
> When they're sorted out on Saturday by us!

They dance

There is a reprise of the last chorus and they finish up collapsed in the two chairs

Black-out

Mrs Brillo and Mrs Rinse exit with the two chairs

A 'chaise longue' or settee and lamp stand are set. On the table is a white cloth, two glasses, an opened bottle of champagne in an ice bucket and a plate of 'things on sticks'

Hidden behind the settee is Daphne with a pad and pen and Benny with an ulcer

The scene is set in one corner of the pitch on a raised area if available

The lighting is pink and seductive. The lamp comes on as the stage lights come up

Song 5b: Incidental 'Musica Romantica'

Sheba enters, humming the tune of the music. She wears an outrageous silky wrap with a feathered collar—it should be some hideous colour like bright orange. She has a huge scent spray which she liberally uses on herself and the audience nearby. She inverts the champagne bottle and puts a dab behind each ear. She is prinking her hair when she hears Norbert's approach

Norbert enters. He has put on his best Hawaiian shirt for the occasion but still sports his flat cap. He enters stealthily and crouches then stops as if outside an imaginary door

Norbert (*whispering*) Mrs S . . .
Sheba Is that you—Tiger?
Norbert (*confused looks behind him*) No—it's Norbert.
Sheba Quickly, Norbert, I'm here.
Norbert There?
Sheba Here—in the office—waiting . . .
Norbert Waiting?
Sheba Yes, waiting—alone.
Norbert Alone?
Sheba Quite, quite—alone.
Norbert I'm coming in then. (*He opens the imaginary door wide*)

Norbert runs into Sheba's arms

Sheba Norbert.
Norbert Yes.
Sheba (*nodding in the door's direction*) The door.
Norbert Oh yeah. (*He goes back and shuts the door*)

Norbert remains by the door

Sheba Fly to my arms—mon brute.
Norbert Coming—ma cherry.

They enfold each other

The following sequence should be delivered quickly

Sheba (*looking into his eyes*) Norbles!
Norbert Sheebles!
Sheba (*offering an already filled glass*) Bubbles?
Norbert Smashles. (*He drinks it down in one*)
Sheba Nibbles? (*She offers a sausage on a stick*)
Norbert Deliciousles. (*He munches it up*)
Sheba (*taking his hand and placing it on her hip*) Caressles?
Norbert (*putting his other hand on her hip*) Cuddles?
Sheba (*taking off his flat cap and fondling his hair*) Fondles?
Norbert (*getting bolder—his hand strays to her bust*) Groples?
Sheba Norbert!

They both look at his hand

(*Treating him like Benny*) Fingers!
Norbert Sorry.
Sheba (*pursing lips*) Liples?
Norbert (*starting to kiss her hand and working up her arm*) Kissles.
Benny (*appearing behind the settee, angrily*) Sizzles!
Daphne (*appearing straight after with her pad*) Scribbles!

Daphne and Benny duck down together

Sheba Norbles come to the window. I want to show you something.

Norbert swallows in expectancy

(*Sliding open an imaginary window*) What do you see outside, Norbles?
Norbert (*looking at the audience*) A lot of strange faces looking at us.
Sheba No Norbert—lower down.
Norbert (*looking at the pitch*) Grass.
Sheba Exactly Norbles—the City ground. My ground—possibly 'our' ground.
Norbert Our ground?
Sheba Yes Norby. You and I—together—we could take City to the top of World football.
Norbert Me—with my superior soccer knowledge.
Sheba Me—with my ravishing beauty.
Norbert We could amalgamate our strengths.
Sheba We could be partners.

Act I

Norbert (*shouting*) Form a concubine!
Sheba Not so loud, Norbert, please. (*She shuts the imaginary window on his fingers*)
Norbert Sorry.
Sheba (*flouncing across to the settee and draping herself on it*) Only one thing holds me back, Norbert. Only one thing prevents me from giving you my all.
Norbert What's that, Sheebles?
Sheba The future, Norbert. What of the future?
Norbert Future?
Sheba Yes—when we've reached the top—after all the tears, torments and traumas.
Norbert The sweat, struggle and strain?
Sheba Yes Norbert. Will you still love me—when I'm old and grey.
Norbert Of course I do!
Benny (*suddenly erupting from behind the settee*) That's it! I've heard enough, already.
Sheba Benjamin!

Daphne leaps up

Norbert Daphne!
Daphne Norbert!
Benny Sheba!
Sheba Benjamin!

Sheba stalks Benny round the settee

How dare you spy on me in the privacy of my office?
Benny (*nervously*) Spy on you.
Daphne (*to Sheba*) You were chattin' 'im up.
Sheba (*turning on her*) Chattin' 'im up! That is absolutely absurd.

Sheba turns back to Benjamin and pins him flat on the settee and leans over him

Typical of your small, jealous little mind, Benjamin. You couldn't have been listening properly or you might have understood everything.
Daphne I've got everything down 'ere, Mrs Shekelstein—(*she shows her the pad*) up to the bit—(*she looks at her notes*) where "you're old and grey".
Sheba (*snatching the pad*) I'll take that, thank you, Daphne!
Norbert I shouldn't jump to conclusions, Mr S.
Benny That's just it, Norbert, I do. You aren't the first you know.
Sheba How disgusting! Just wait till I get you home, Benjamin. Listening in. Prying. Poking your big nose into my affairs.
Norbert We were making a selfless effort to pull City out of the mire.
Benny And how exactly were you going to do that?
Sheba (*relieved; picking up a glass*) Tell him how we were going to do it, Norbert.
Norbert (*lost and jumping at any idea*) Er—buy a new player.
Sheba (*double takes*) Buy a new player—are you sure that's what we discussed, Norbert?

Norbert (*more confidently*) Yes, we definitely decided to spend capital on a new star player.
Benny Well, that certainly makes sense.
Sheba (*icily*) And—how much did *we* decide to spend, Norbert? (*She drinks*)
Norbert A hundred and twenty thousand pounds.
Sheba (*choking and spitting 'champers' out of her mouth*) What!
Norbert Less ten per cent for Club coach's commission.
Sheba You are learning fast, Norbert.
Daphne Well done, Norbert.
Benny Very well, if that is what your discussion was about—I might possibly, in my passionate uncontrollable jealousy, have misconceived your motives, Sheba.
Daphne But where are we going to find a 'class player' at this time of the season?
Benny Pertinent point, Daphne. Do you really think, Norbert, that just by magic someone is going to suddenly appear right under our very noses?

Joe sweeps in with his trolley and skids to a halt

Joe One lump or two?
Daphne A miracle.
Sheba Don't be stupid, Daphne.
Norbert That's just the tea-boy.
Benny We need a star.
Sheba For a hundred and twenty thousand we'd want a superstar.
Daphne Someone who could do everything.
Norbert Like play football.

A football is thrown into the area which Joe immediately juggles with doing astonishing tricks keeping the ball in the air with his foot, head etc.

Benny He's good!
Sheba Someone who could dance.

Joe traps the ball, leaves it where it is and walks to a new spot. He stands—there is a moment—he shuffles his feet quickly like a tap dancer with percussion accompaniment

Daphne Fantastic!
Benny Someone who could sing.

Joe moves to near the keyboard of the band and just sings badly the one word of a well-known song

Joe (*singing*) Moonriver.
Norbert Brilliant!
Daphne Someone who can make love.
Sheba Daphne!

Joe moves over to Daphne takes her in his arms and kisses her very quickly

Daphne is left frozen and transfixed with pleasure

Act I

Norbert Someone who can score goals.

Joe dribbles the trapped ball towards goal then smacks it in the back of the net

All (*except frozen Daphne*) Goal!!

They all descend on Joe to congratulate him

Norbert waves a contract

Benny (*shaking Joe's hand*) You're a good boy, Joe.
Joe Ta.
Sheba (*offering her hand*) You have the qualities I'm searching for.
Joe (*kissing her hand*) Oh—more ta's.
Norbert We want you to read this contract carefully—(*He holds it in front of Joe*)

They all read it making 'fast' reading noises. They stop, turn it over and make the same noises until they reach the bottom of the page

   and sign it.
Daphne (*coming to her senses, running over*) You can use my pen.
Joe Where do I sign?
Sheba Benjamin.

They all look at Benjamin

   Finger!

Benny points his finger and then swoops it up to descend on the dotted line of the contract

Joe signs

Benny Excellent. You are now on the pay roll of City F.C.
Daphne As a first team player.
Joe Blimey—Joe Rabbit—a somebody.
Daphne That'll please Sylv.
Norbert (*patting him on the back*) You'll be in City colours tomorrow, lad.
Daphne And get a cheque for—(*she looks at the contract*) a hundred and twenty thousand pounds.
Norbert Less ten per cent for Club coach's commission.
Sheba (*snatching the contract—she didn't need reminding of the money*) Thank you, Daphne.
Joe I can't believe it.
Benny Start believing it, son.
Norbert See you at the ground Wednesday night, Joe.
Sheba When you'll start earning that money.

Benny mimes the feel of the money

   Benjamin!

They all look at Benjamin

   Fingers!

Benny (*stopping*) Sorry, dear.
Sheba See that this scenery is moved away. (*She points to the office set*)
Benny Yes, dear.
Sheba Norbert—come and help me change.
Norbert Yes, dear.
Sheba Daphne!
Daphne Yes, dear?
Sheba Go and wash your neck—it's filthy!

Sheba exits with Norbert

Daphne (*change phrase as required*) Tit-face!

Daphne exits in the opposite direction

The groundstaff enter and exit with Benny. They remove everything except the settee and the lamp

Joe (*calling off*) Sylv!
Sylv (*off stage*) What?
Joe Wotcher doin'?
Sylv (*off stage*) Me hair. Why?
Joe Well, leave it in the basin and come down here.

Sylv enters, with a towel round her head

Sylv Wot's up?
Joe I–am—a—star.
Sylv Is—that—all. (*She goes to leave*)
Joe (*running in front of her to stop her*) No, Sylv. Serious. Sheba has just signed me for City.
Sylv You're jokin'!
Joe No jokes. I've signed for one hundred and twenty thousand smackers.
Sylv So you're in the cup side on Wednesday against Bruddersford?
Joe That's right.
Sylv Who's been dropped, then?
Joe No one, Tubs has got a three match suspension.
Sylv What for?
Joe Making faces at the ref.
Sylv What?
Joe Wiv his fingers.
Sylv Oh. So no more worries now, eh Joe?
Joe Well, there is one thing worrying me.
Sylv What's that?
Joe Well, it's confusin' me really.
Sylv Confusing you?
Joe I'm not very good at the old maffermatics.
Sylv Wotcher talkin' about, Joe?
Joe Well, it's that hundred and twenty thousand quid.
Sylv What about it?
Joe Well, if *you* were offered a hundred and twenty thousand quid, Sylv, *less* ten percent—how much would you take off?

Act I 33

Sylv (*thinking for a moment*) Everything—except me earrings!

They laugh

                Song 6: A Little Bit of Me (Reprise)

Joe and Sylv   Both of us have got it
                     And we've got a lot of it
                     We've got a lot of what it takes
                     And if we want a bit of it
                     Just a little bit
                     We won't muck about.
                     Just say that
                     We'd like a little bit
                     Just a little bit
                     We'd like a little bit of...

(*Speaking*)   One hundred and twenty thousand quid!

Joe and Sylv collapse exhausted onto the settee together

Sylv You know what's happened, don't yer, Joe?
Joe (*thinking she means love*) No—You tell me, Sylv.
Sylv I've just sat on Gazza!
Joe Oh no!

Black-out, including the lamp

Sylv and Joe exit with the settee and the lamp

The Lights come up as floodlights. Wednesday night

The police and the groundstaff enter

Loudspeaker Welcome to City football ground for this return match against Bruddersford United. City lost their recent league match against the Northern side but hope to reverse that result this evening in the quarter finals of the six-a-side championship. Bruddersford on their way to the quarter finals have defeated Spurs, Manchester United and Liverpool while City have had—three byes. There is just one change in your printed programme. For City, Tubs is suspended——

Cheers off stage

——and tonight the number six shirt will be worn by new signing—Joe Rabbit.

Big cheers off stage

Tonight's lucky programme number is twenty-seven and the winner may collect tonight's matchball signed by all the City Players at the end of the evening's performance from——
And now let's hear it for City!

The supporters enter

Supporters (*Clap-clap: clap-clap-clap: clap-clap-clap-clap*) City!
(*Clap-clap: clap-clap-clap: clap-clap-clap-clap*) City!
(*Clap-clap: clap-clap-clap: clap-clap-clap-clap*) City!

Song 7: City (reprise)

City City
Isn't it a pity
You can't tell
Yer left foot from yer right!
Yer shootin's hit'n'miss
'Arf the time yer Brahms and Liszt
And you 'aven't scored a goal fer sixteen weeks!
City! City!
Where's yer nitty-gritty?
You must really try and give it some
Start dishin' out the dirties
Hack their shins and rip their shirties
Yes, just get us off
The bottom of the league!

The supporters move to the edge of the pitch and repeat the Clap sequence as they move

Music: 7a

Loudspeaker And here they come. It's the red and white wizards. It's City!

The City team run in as for the opening sequence—but they look more confident

Joe actually looks and moves like a footballer

And tonight's visitors. The boys from the Blackstuff! Bruddersford United.

There are boos from the supporters as:

Bruddersford enter, running. They intimidate as before

The referee enters blowing his whistle—one blast for each step. He places the ball in the centre and blows his whistle for kick off

In slow motion the Bruddersford team take swings at their opposite numbers but the City players duck then punch the Bruddersford team in the stomach. They, in turn, with hideous groans, collapse to the floor

Cue for music for "Boot Song" and normal speed for the players

Music 7b: Hokey Cokey

The City players sing the song and carry out the actions on the Bruddersford players on the floor. The Song is done in double time

Act I   35

Shaky attacks a non-existent player

While the Bruddersford goalie prepares for Joe Rabbit who has dribbled the ball to a point about two yards from goal

Joe (*addressing the goalie*) One lump or two?
Goalie Two.
Joe (*giving the goalie two thumps*) One-two.

The goalie collapses, while the rest freeze and Joe speaks

Joe's got the ball. (*He puts his foot on the ball*)
Team (*echoing*) Joe's got the ball.
Joe Joe's goin' to shoot. (*He brings his foot back*)
Team Joe's going to shoot.
Joe Joe's shot!
Team Goal!

This time it's the Bruddersford team that limp off the pitch, disgraced

Joe is carried off in triumph by his team

The City management enter, with Daphne carrying some newspapers

Sheba Magnificent.
Benny Fantastic.
Norbert Magic.
Sylv That's my Joe!
Daphne I thought they showed off really.
Sheba Don't be stupid, Daphne.
Daphne Sorry, Mrs Shekelstein.
Sheba Following this cup triumph we must call an emergency——

The groundstaff enter with four chairs and the table, under the table, on a shelf is a box marked, 'Sound Effects'

Groundstaff (*plonking down the table*) Board Meeting.
Sheba Right. So please draw up your——
Groundstaff Chairs! (*They arrange the chairs*)

The groundstaff exit

Sheba Right. This, gentlemen, is a red-letter day for City F.C. Newspapers, please, Daphne.
Daphne (*holding them ready*) *Playboy*, *Penthouse* or *The Guardian*?
Sheba *The Guardian* will do thank you.
Daphne Right. (*She puts it down*) I'll put the others in your office, as usual, Mr Shekelstein.

They all turn slowly and look disapprovingly at Benny

Benny (*appealing*) I like the crosswords.

Daphne exits with the remaining papers

Sheba Now, let's see who we've drawn in the semi-finals. Norbert. (*She passes him the newspaper*)

Norbert (*trying to read it*) I can't read it. I'm too excited.

Daphne enters

Sylv (*spotting Daphne returning*) Let Daphne read it.
Sheba Daphne. (*She passes her the paper*)
Daphne Right. (*She puts on her glasses*) Let me see—here we are. Stop Press. Results of the World six-a-side quarter finals. City F.C. one/ Bruddersford United nil. That's us. We've won!
Sheba God, give me strength.
Sylv We know that Daphne. Who have we drawn in the semi-final?
Daphne Oh yeah, here it is. The winner of the City-Bruddersford match will play the winner—of the other match.
Sheba Heaven preserve us, the girl's an imbecile!
Norbert (*patiently*) So, Daphne, what was the result of the other match?
Daphne Oh yeah, here it is—Unreal Madrid—two; Beaujolais Rangers—fourteen!
Sylv Blimey we've drawn the frogs.
Benny We're into Europe!
Sheba Home or away?
Daphne (*reading*) "The match to be played at the Stade de Fromage, Paris".
Sylv Paris. How romantic! I'll have to get Gazza some travel sickness tablets.
Daphne Why?
Sylv He's been feeling a bit flat lately.
Daphne Oh.
Norbert Beaujolais. There's no way we'll beat them out there. They've got the best coach in Europe.
Benny Maurice Le Fleur?
Norbert Right first time, Benny.
Sheba We'll find a way, Norbert. It's just a question of planning.
Benny When do we fly out?
Sylv Friday morning.
Daphne That's ages yet.
Sylv No, the time'll flash by.

Music: 7c

Loudspeaker The Friday morning departure for Paris leaves in two minutes time.
Sylv There you are—what did I tell you?
Loudspeaker All passengers and the City football club are asked to ensure that their baggage has been checked before boarding Air France economy flight *un, deux, trois*.
Sheba (*producing a box marked 'Sound Effects'. There is a large red button on the top*) Benjamin.

They all look at Benjamin

Finger!

Act I   37

Benny presses down the red button and immediately we hear the sound of the plane taking off

The Lights fade to darkness

In the darkness we hear squeals of excitement and bustle

  The groundstaff enter and exit with the table and chairs

The Lights come up as:

  The City team, Benny, Sylv, Norbert, Sheba and Daphne enter with travel bags etc.

Music 7d: Incidental French Cafe Music

Benny We've arrived.
Sylv Paris.
Einstein Look! (*He points*)

They all look

  The Trifle tower.
Titch Cor, innit big!
Joe Course it is.
Titch Why?
Joe It's a Gallic symbol, innit?
All Oh yeah.
Speaker de loude Welcome to Paree, City Football Club. May we introduce to you your host and the fabulous manager of the famous Rangers de Beaujolais, Monsieur Maurice Le Fleur!

There is music as:

  The girls of the Beaujolais team run in and form a kind of guard of honour for Maurice Le Fleur. One of them carries a boater and another a cane

  Maurice Le Fleur enters to applause and there is a great deal of blowing of kisses to the audience and his team. He spots Benny and makes towards him — kissing him on both cheeks

Maurice Monsieur Ben-ja-min. I am so plaisired to meet vous.
Benny (*taken aback by the kissing*) Plaisired to meet vous, already.
Maurice (*spotting Sheba*) And this must be your *most* charmant wife?
Benny No, it's the only one I've got.

Maurice kisses Sheba's hand, which she loves

Lofty Oi Guvnor. Who's that lot over there? (*He points to the Rangers team*)
Maurice (*echoing in cockney*) That lot over there — I mean — zat lot over zere? Why, zat is my team — zee Beaujolais Rangers. Give them a wave lovely lads.
Rangers Ooo La La. (*They all wave*)
Enid (*moving towards them*) I want a transfer.
Norbert Enid. Behave yourself.

Norbert pulls Enid back

Maurice Oh, you naughty English! You are—ow you say, so——
Einstein Thick?
Maurice *Exactement.* But what am I zinkin' off? You are in Paris. A city of excitement and magique. Please walk zis way. (*He walks across the area in a camp manner*)

The City team and the City management copy his walk exactly

The groundstaff enter

Maurice Please be seated.

The team and management form a tight group—you can use the groundstaff on hands and knees as seats

And now, pour vous, un petite tour of our lovely city. And your guide shall be——
Rangers Maurice le Fleur.
Maurice Cue music!

Two of the Rangers girls hand Maurice a cane and a Maurice Chevalier boater

Song 8: Maurice Le Fleur

Beaujolais Rangers	Welcome to Paris
	La plume de ma tante
	Welcome to Paris
	Comment allez-vous.
	Welcome to Paris
	Ooo la la—oui oui
	Welcome to Paris
	To Gay Paree.
Maurice	Let me be your guide
	Monsieur Maurice Le Fleur
	Let me show you Versailles
	And the Folies Bergere
	I'm known throughout France
	All my friends know my name
	Just check with the vicaire
	At la Madeleine.
Beaujolais Rangers	Maurice Maurice
	Tout le monde loves Maurice
	He's the flower of Paree
	He's naughty, he's saucy
	He's oh such a card
	People come from miles to see
	His grand boulevard.
Maurice	Let me be your friend
	Monsieur Maurice Le Fleur
	We'll dine late at Maxims

Act I   39

	Drink in gay Fontainebleau
	My taste is superb
	I'm an expert on booze
	A night out with me would turn
	Your *moulin* quite rouge!
Rangers Team and	Maurice Maurice
Management	Tout le monde loves Maurice
	He's the pansy of Paree
	He likes you
	He wants you
	And if you don't join
	People say he'll kick you
	Up the Bois de Boulogne
Maurice	Let me be your friend
	Monsieur Maurice Le Fleur
	We'll travel the Metro
	Walk the park Luxembourg
	We'll visit the Lido
	And then Montparnasse
	Just think of the naughty things
	We'll do on the bus!
All	Maurice Maurice
	Tout le monde loves Maurice
	He's the pot plant of Paree
	He's saucy, he's naughty
	He's oh such a sport
	Like your Larry Grayson
	He says "Fermez la Porte"
	So welcome to Paris
	La plume de ma tante
	Welcome to Paris
	Comment allez-vous
	Welcome to Paris
	Welcome to Paris
	Welcome to Paris
	To gay Paree!

At the end of the number the naughty Beaujolais Rangers team trip off the area then pause and look back at the City team

Rangers (*in unison*) Désirez-vous un tour de Paree?
City Team Not arf!
Rangers On votre bicycles, then!

The City team and Norbert follow the Rangers off

Maurice And now, I shall 'ave a natter confidential avec Monsieur Sodastream.
Benny Shekelstein!

Benny moves across to Maurice leaving Sylv, Sheba and Daphne listening in

Maurice Oui. Je understand that votre team, le City, are très weak.
Benny Mon team?
Maurice *Oui*, je understand that they are un shower de layabouts.
Benny How dare vous. Ils sont fantastic.
Maurice Really, in Paris we call them the 'Premiere Poofteurs'
Benny That is le straw finale. One more insult like that sunshine and je will rearrange votre features.
Maurice Ha! (*He pushes his face into Benny's face*) Allez-stuffed!
Benny And up votres.

Benny gives Maurice the 'V' sign as:

  Maurice exits

Sheba Benjamin.

They all look at Benny

  Fingers!
Benny Sorry dear.

  Benny exits

Daphne I fink we're gonna lose this one, Mrs S.
Sheba Defeat is not a word in my vocabulary, Daphne.
Daphne No?
Sheba No.
Sylv Joe can beat 'em.
Sheba Joe is a fine player but this team will be a hard nut to crack without some strategy.
Daphne (*excitedly to the audience*) She's got a plan.
Sheba I've got a plan.
Daphne (*to the audience*) Told yer.
Sheba We must be realistic. There is no way we can defeat the froggies on this—their home ground—so we must force a replay.
Sylv How can we force a replay?
Daphne Ask them nicely?
Sheba They're frogs, Daphne. They don't know the meaning of the word "nice". No we must do it legally.
Sylv You mean . . .?
Sheba Exactly. Get the game abandoned and force them to play the return on the hallowed turf of——

They stand to attention

  Wembley.
Sylv How can we get it abandoned?
Sheba By doing what all true blue Brits do when their backs are against the wall.
Daphne Have a riot!
Sheba Have a gigantic riot.
Sylv Yeah! 'Ere but hold on—who's goin' to raid the pitch?
Sheba Who? WHO? (*She turns to the audience and points*) Why *them*!

… Act I   41

Music 8a: Land of Hope and Glory

This few, this happy few. This band of brothers.
Daphne Our loyal fans.
Sheba Yes, our loyal fans who have travelled with us across the seas.
Sylv The scourge of the Sally Line. Never flinching.
Sheba Steadfast and true!
Daphne The red, white and blue.

The supporters enter

Sheba I call upon you now. You stout hearts. Will you hold aloft your trusty aggro bags. That's it! Higher, so all France can see them.
Sylv Wave them!
Daphne Shake them!
Sheba Stamp your feet!
Sylv Give us a C!
Audience and **supporters** 'C'.
Sylv Give us an I!
Audience and **supporters** 'I'.
Daphne Give us a B!
Sylv A 'T', you berk!
Daphne Oh yeah. Give us a T!
Audience and **supporters** 'T'.
Daphne Give us a Y!
Audience and **supporters** 'Y'.
All Give us City!
Audience and **supporters** 'City'!

Sheba raises her arms for silence

Sheba Whisper! Right up to Beaujolais!
Audience (*whispering*) Right up to Beaujolais!
Sylv Shout, "Death to the frogs!"
Audience Death to the frogs!
Daphne Scream, "We're with the Woolwich!"
Audience We're with the Woolwich!
Sheba Excellent. We are now at fever pitch. Don't let me down. Remember if the French score this pitch must be raided. I want this field awash with debris. Load up with ammo from your aggro bags.

The audience do so

Pulverise their players.
Sylv Mash up their management.
Speaker de loude Madames et Messieurs, welcome to Le Stade de Fromage pour semi-final de la six-a-side championship du monde. Votre teams are as per programme. Et ici est le team fabulous. Le Rangers de Beaujolais.

The audience boo as:

The Beaujolais Rangers run on

Et maintenant le team de uncouth pigs—Le City Anglais.

The audience applaud

The City team enters

Zee referee for the match from Allemande, Herr Vistlekraut.

Herr Vistlekraut enters

The two teams line up

The French police and the St Joan's ambulance madames enter

Vistlekraut (*addressing the two teams*) Gentlemenz vee will play zis game accordink to zee rules of football. I don't vant any dirty tricks or funny bizness. Now, let us be shakink zee hands unt greeting.

The City team shakes hands with the Beaujolais side, who are girls, remember? They kiss the City players in the French fashion. The City lads like that and take it a bit further until the two teams are in clinches everywhere. This should be funny rather than romantic. Enid slaps his partner's wrists for instance, while Shaky can't find his partner although he is making kissing sounds and searching for her

Herr Vistlekraut blows his whistle stridently for order. He is livid

Vistlekraut Vot are you doink! Vot is zis!! You all acting like Lady Chatterbags lover! Stop all zis feelzee muckink about—unt play! (*He blows his whistle*)

The match starts. The French team are good. Herr Vistlekraut follows the ball everywhere, his nose nearly on the ball. The French leave the City players sprawling as they pass beautifully. Eventually the ball comes to Marcel Morceau who bangs the ball in the back of the net

Sheba Britons to arms! Attack!

The supporters and the audience bombard the field and start fighting with the French Police and St Joan's Ambulance madames

The French team exit, running and screaming "Sacha Distel lives", etc.

Herr Vistlekraut is laid out

There are punch ups everywhere

Song 9: But We'll Support Yer (City reprise)

Supporters   "We'll be out there in the crowd, etc."

The House Lights come up on total devastation

The arena is cleared during the interval by City staff

ACT II

Second Half. Afternoon. Wembley

On stage is a raised block

As the audience return, music is playing and the groundstaff have already started to filter on to the area

The supporters can be heard off stage

Loudspeaker Welcome to Wembley Stadium on this glorious afternoon for the semi-final replay of the World six-a-side Championship. But just before the kick-off I want you all to put your hands together and give a warm welcome to our very own Joe Rabbit, who is going to lead us in the time-honoured community singing. Joe Rabbit—ladies and gentlemen!

There is applause and cheers from the supporters and the audience as:

Joe Rabbit enters in a white suit with his football kit underneath it

Joe Thank you. Thank you. (*He waves to the crowd and then leaps up onto the raised block*) And now, ladies and gentlemen could we have complete silence—absolute quiet.

It goes suddenly quiet

Well not quite as quiet as that but quite quiet. This afternoon I'm going to sing a song especially written for the occasion by yours truly—Joe Rabbit. A little number entitled "When You Walk on a Frog". (*He turns to the keyboard player*) Thank you maestro!

The supporters echo the italicized words three times, the upper case words six times and the asterisked word twelve times

Song 9b: When You Walk on a Frog

When you *walk* on a *frog*
Lift your *boots* up *high*
And *don't* be *afraid* of the DENTS
At the *end* of the *fight*
Is a *fifty* quid *fine*
And a *six* monthly *stretch* in the NICK
So walk *on* through the *wind*
Walk *on* through the *rain*
And you'll never walk ALONE (LONE, LONE . . .)
You'll never walk alone.*

There is applause from the supporters

Thank you very much. And now—it's your turn. And as we sing this great song I want you to unfold your programmes and hold them up high. Right up. That's it. Right up above your head. I want all those people at home watching the TV to see what a marvellous time we're having here this afternoon. Right here we go and I'll help you with the words.

The supporters enter and unfold their programmes and are encouraging the audience to do the same. There should be a sea of red and white

Joe gives each line to the audience and then they sing it. As the audience sings the last word of each line Joe shouts out the next line—or the lines may be on a song-sheet or projected

Joe, supporters   When you *walk* on a *frog*
and audience   Lift your *boots* up *high*
                         And *don't* be afraid of the DENTS
                         At the *end* of the *fight*
                         Is a *fifty* quid *fine*
                         And a *six* monthly *stretch* in the NICK.
                         So walk *on* through the *wind*
                         Walk *on* through the *rain*
                         And you'll never walk ALONE
                         You'll never walk alone.*

Joe That's really marvellous. And now can we hear it for Beaujolais Rangers?
Supporters (*very short, sharp and fast*) Boo!
Joe And now for City!
Supporters (*Clap-clap: clap-clap-clap: clap-clap-clap-clap*) City!
Joe And now sadly it's time for me to say goodbye—but before I go can I ask all our fans to try and forget that nasty business in Paris involving the two linesmen and the can of petrol and welcome in true Wembley fashion Her Majesty the Queen on this right royal occasion!

The two teams enter and form groups either side of the area

The supporters take their places on the pitch. The teams sing and have static, choreographed movements while the supporters sing and dance

Song 10: Right Royal Occasion

Supporters and **Teams**   On this right royal occasion
                               There's a right royal request
                               That every fan at Wembley here
                               Puts on his Sunday best
                               Roll out the royal carpet
                               Unfurl the royal flag
                               And give a cheer for
                               Pickles and beer
                               And the lady we love best.

Act II

Wot a day!
City's into Europe
Wot a day!
We're gonna win the cup, cup, cup
Wot a day!
I really can't believe it
Cos' after three
The booze is free
And all the pubs
Will give away grub
Birds up the manor
Cost only a tanner
The world's gone bleedin' mad
So give a cheer for
Pickles and beer
And the lady we love best.

On this right royal occasion
There's a right royal plea
That every fan at Wembley here
Goes to the Queen's for tea
Get out the royal teapot
Lay out the royal nosh
And give a shout
For cockles and stout
And the lady we love best.

Wot a day!
City's into Europe
Wot a day!
We're gonna win the cup, cup, cup.
Wot a day!
I really can't believe it.
Cos' after three
The booze is free
And all the pubs
Will give away grub
Birds up the manor
Cost only a tanner
They even say
The coppers are gay
And mother-in-laws
Are droppin' their drawers
The world's gone bleedin' mad
So give a cheer
For pickles and beer
And the lady we love
Lady we love
Lady we love best!
Oi!

When the song ends, the supporters exit with excited whispers of "Here she comes"

Sheba, Benny, Norbert, Daphne and Sylv enter. They are in their glad rags, except Norbert and Daphne who has her pad and pen with her, to meet the Queen. They line up to be presented

The teams line up in front of their respective goals

Music: 10

The Queen enters to regal music dragging a lump of fur or shaggy carpet (her royal corgi) attached to a piece of elastic

Sheba Your Majesty (*She curtsies*)

The Queen ignores her

Benny Your Majesty. (*He holds out his hand and inadvertently steps onto the corgi and traps it there*)

The Queen ignores him

Sylv Your Majesty (*She bows*)

The Queen ignores her and goes directly to Daphne

Queen Daphne how nice to see you.

The Queen shakes Daphne's hand

Daphne Could I have your autograph?

The City team frantically try to attract Benny's attention

Queen Most certainly.
Daphne (*handing her the pad*) Just here under Madonna.

The Queen scribbles her name

Norbert (*raising his cap*) Your Majesty may I introduce the City Football team?
Queen Delighted. (*She moves across to the team lined up*)

Titch is completely hidden by the others

Benny stands on the corgi-elastic at full stretch

   Albert!

Benny releases the corgi and it zips across the stage

Norbert This is our skipper, Lofty.
Queen Lawfty? Charming.
Lofty Thank you, ma'm.
Queen And what do you do, Lawfty?
Lofty I'm a footballer, ma'm.
Queen (*amazed*) A footballer?
Lofty Yes, ma'am.

Act II

Queen So that means you—er ...
Lofty Play football, ma'am.
Queen Play football. Most interesting.
Norbert This is one of our attackers, ma'am, Titch.

Titch tries to poke his head through the team

Queen Where is he?
Norbert Down there, ma'm.

The players make a gap for Titch to squeeze through

Queen So he is. Hallo, little chap.
Titch 'Allo.
Queen And what do you do, Titch?
Titch I'm a footballer, ma'm.
Queen A footballer? So that means you—er ...
Titch Play football, ma'm.
Queen Excellent.
Norbert Enid, your Majesty. Defence.
Enid (*curtseying*) I'm a footballer as well, ma'm.
Queen (*amazed*) Another footballer! So that means you—er ...
Enid Play football, ma'am.
Queen Marvellous. You know, you should get together with Lawfty and Titch and play with them. They're footballers as well you know.

They look confused

Norbert Shaky the Goalkeeper.
Shaky I'm a far ... far ... footballer as well, ma'm.
Queen Does he always stutter?
Norbert Only when he speaks, ma'm.
Queen Wonderful.
Norbert Tubs, ma'm.
Queen (*shaking hands*) Tubs. And what do you do?
Tubs Well, I do a very nice line in battery clocks, Taiwan wrist watches——
Norbert No Tubs, Her Majesty means what are you doing today?
Tubs Oh—er I'm playing football.
Queen (*amazed*) Good Heavens! What a lot of footballers all in one place! Quite extraordinary. How long have you been playing Tubs?
Tubs 'Bout two years, ma'm.
Queen Goodness. You must be quite exhausted.

There is a pause

City team (*realizing*) Oh yeah (*Looking at the others*) Royal joke.

The City team all give a short, sharp laugh

Norbert Einstein, ma'm.
Queen Hallo Einstein. Tell me, Einstein, why is your hair parted down the middle in that unusual manner.
Einstein It keeps my brain evenly balanced, ma'm.
Queen What a first class idea—I must tell Charles about it.

Norbert Joe Rabbit.
Queen Ah, now you're that star player, right Joe?
Joe So they tell me, ma'm
Norbert He can hit a ball like a rocket with either foot.
Queen Really? Oh I do envy you, Joe. You know I think I'd give my right leg to be ambidextrous.

There is a pause

(*Looking at the others*) Royal joke!

City team (*realising*) Oh yeah! (*Short, sharp laugh*)
Queen Now, after I've been introduced to the frogs—I shall go up there to my little seat while you all go and kick your balls about—but before I leave—er——
Norbert Norbert, ma'm.
Queen But before I leave, Norbert, may I thank you for being so interesting.

The Queen waves to the City team

The City team wave back

She walks the length of the pitch dragging her corgi with her towards the Beaujolais side

Maurice (*bowing and kissing the Queen's hand*) Your Majesty.

At this the Queen clouts Maurice round the chops and then proceeds to belabour the Beaujolais players with her handbag—belting and kicking them in a variety of their anatomical regions. This is accompanied by percussive rim-shots etc. She acts in a most unregal manner but having demolished them we hear the regal music again and she returns to her cool self. She sits waving to the crowd leaving a pile of devastated players behind her

Queen God bless you all. Buy British. Send a gunboat!

Music: 10b

The Queen exits to applause

Herr Vistlekraut enters blowing his whistle in the usual fashion

The teams drift to their place

The Beaujolais team limp to their positions after the royal onslaught

Herr Vistlekraut I von't no repercustards of vat happened in Europe. Zat game vas unt complete 'arse!'
Joe (*correcting his English*) Farce!
Herr Vistlekraut Farce! No hooliganisms. Play zee game accordink to zee rools! It's animals like you vot start verld vars! (*He blows his whistle*)

There is no slow motion this time

The City side go straight into the hokey-cokey treatment

Act II   49

Song 10c: Hokey Cokey

City team   You put your left boot in
　　　　　　　Your left boot out
　　　　　　　In-out-in-out
　　　　　　　You boot 'em all about
　　　　　　　You do the cobbler crunching
　　　　　　　And you nut'em quick
　　　　　　　Cos that's what it's all about!

The Beaujolais players are left in agony on the floor

Joe dribbles the ball to the goal

Joe Joe's got the ball. (*He puts his foot on the ball*)

The Beaujolais team freeze

City team Joe's got the ball.
Joe Joe's goin' to shoot. (*He puts his foot back*)
City team Joe's goin' to shoot.
Joe Joe's shot. (*He hits the ball into the back of the net*)
City team and the **City Supporters** GOAL!

While the City supporters give three rhythmic claps

　Maurice exits in tears

　The Beaujolais players limp off after him

　Two white-coated hospital attendants enter and take Herr Vistlekraut to a funny farm

　The City team carry Joe off shoulder high

The management hurry forward

Sheba Majestic!
Benny Regal!
Norbert Classic!
Sylv Real pedigree!
Daphne I thought the Queen mucked about too much.
Sheba Don't be stupid, Daphne.
Daphne Sorry.

　Joe enters running in a track suit

Joe Well, what didjer fink of the game, Sylv?
Sylv Terrific, Joe.
Norbert Great, son.
Joe Wasn't bad was it? I fink a little celebration is called for. (*He whistles*)

　Mrs Brillo and Mrs Rinse enter wearing their supporters scarves and favours. They are pushing Joe's old tea-trolley now with a smart white cloth. There is champagne in five glasses, an empty glass, a bottle in an ice-bucket and three bouquets

Sylv What's this, Joe?
Sheba Looks expensive whatever it is.
Joe Don't panic Mrs S. This is a little surprise out of me first week's wages.
Daphne Ooo lovely.

Mrs Brillo and Mrs Rinse hand out the drinks but they do not have a glass for Benny

Joe Flowers for the lovely ladies.

Joe gives the bouquets to Sylv, Sheba and Daphne

Daphne It's like Harvest Festival.
Joe Norbert—a toast!
Norbert Right—er—to City!
All To City! (*They all drink*)

Benny raises an empty hand fractionally after the others

Benny City!
Norbert And the World Cup!
All And the World Cup!!

Mrs Brillo and Mrs Rinse each take a swig from the bottle

Benny World Cup.
Joe That'll be all ladies, thank you. (*He takes the bottle*)
Mrs Brillo Not quite, Joe.
Joe Why, what else is there?
Mrs Rinse Yer socks——
Mrs Brillo Fer soakin——
Mrs Rinse In the suds——
Mrs Brillo On Saturday.
Joe Oh, yeah, course. (*He pulls his socks out of the top of his track suit bottoms*) Here we are.

Mrs Brillo grabs them in ecstasy

  Hildegard!
Mrs Brillo Yes Joe?
Joe One each.
Mrs Brillo Oh yeah. (*She hands one to Mrs Rinse*)

  Mrs Brillo and Mrs Rinse exit gleefully

Sheba Talking of the World Cup—who are the other finalists?
Daphne It's all right. I remembered this time. I looked up the result in the paper and wrote it down on a bit of paper.
Sheba And?
Daphne I lost the bit of paper.
Joe Don't flap, Daphne, they announced the final draw on the telly straight after the Beaujolais game.
Benny Who've we got?
Joe The Mexican champions.

Act II   51

Norbert Blimey—not——
Joe Right. Chi Hua Hua Academicals!
Sylv We'll never beat them.
Sheba We'll deal with that problem when it arrives. Our most immediate problem is that a trip to Mexico will place an unnecessary burden on our financial resources.
Norbert We'll need to raise extra cash, like?
Sheba Concise, as always, dear Norbert.
Sylv (*with a sudden brainwave*) Couldn't we raise the extra cash by running more social events down at the—whatjercall it—the—wotsit place?
Joe The Supporters Club?
Sylv You know—where all the City followers go after the game.
Joe That's the Supporters Club.
Sylv Where they hold all the dances and bingo in the evenings.
Joe You mean the Supporters Club.
Sylv What do you call it?
Joe The Supporters Club!
Sylv That's it—the Supporters Club.
Joe (*to the audience*) And I'm thinkin' of marrying this!
Benny We'll need more than just money raised by the Supporters Club.
Sheba We must increase the entrance money at the gate.
Benny To what?
Sheba Ten pounds.
Benny Ten pounds! Blimey I could get a good woman for that price.
Joe Not for forty-five minutes each way, you couldn't.

There is a pause

Daphne And a band playing at half-time.
Joe Look you're all up Willesden Junction. Increased turnstile prices won't work.
Sylv What would you suggest then, Joe?
Joe Well if I wanted to increase the gate—I'd improve City's image.
Norbert Improve the image.
Joe That's right. Sell City to the public by advertising on the old telly.
Sheba Joe, despite the fact that at times you bear a close affinity to some bizarre Walt Disney creation, I think you might have hit on a colourful and lucrative idea.
Joe What's she mean?
Sylv She likes it.
Joe Oh, good.
Sheba Benjamin. Ring the Golden Ball Advertising Agency immediately.
Benny Certainly dear—er—I haven't got a phone.
Sheba Well don't just stand there—improvise!

Benny mimes a phone and does stupid phoning gestures when after a couple of seconds Norbert opens his jacket to reveal a 'trimphone' attached to the lining of his coat

Benny picks up the phone but is not too sure what to do next

Sheba Benjamin!

They all look at Benny

Finger!
Benny (*looking at a finger*) Oh yes! (*He uses the finger to dial*) Golden Ball Advertising agency?
Voice (*offstage or through a loudspeaker; very sultry*) Y-e-s.
Benny We want to book all available studio space to shoot a soccer special entitled—er——
Daphne (*speaking before Sheba has a chance*) "City. My City".
Benny Entitled "City. My City".
Voice When do you want to start shooting?
Benny And we want to start shooting—er——
Daphne (*speaking before Sheba again*) Straight away.
Benny Straight away.
Voice L-o-v-e-l-y.

Benny replaces the phone

Sheba Norbert, round up the team from the jacuzzi and explain our plans.
Norbert Yes, Mrs S.
Sheba (*sotto voce*) Oh, and Norbert, immediately after the TV Special I would like to see you at the La Gropa Dancing Academy. Privately.
Benny I heard that—don't you start any more hanky panky.
Sheba Purely business arrangements, Benjamin. Don't be so childish. Now let's get ready.
Sylv I'll give Gazza a brush.

Sylv exits

Norbert I'll change me cap.

Norbert exits

Benny I'll polish me wallet.

Benny exits

Joe (*starting to exit*) I'll write a few jingles for the commercial.
Daphne (*starting to exit*) And I'll sharpen me pencil.
Sheba Don't bother, Daphne. You—aren't—going—anywhere.
Daphne But the television—and thingies.

Joe has stopped to listen

Sheba You certainly don't think I'm going to allow something like you within a mile of an advert for the City Club, do you?
Daphne Why not?
Sheba Why not? Because you're a walking disaster, Daphne, that's why not. Because you're scruffy, stupid and about as physically attractive as a punctured football.
Daphne You don't like me, do you?

Act II

Sheba I don't like you one bit, Daphne. And you are not going to the Golden Ball!

Joe That's a bit hard, Mrs S.

Sheba (*turning on Joe*) Rabbit, if you wish to continue earning your green lettuce at this club and have any aspirations concerning my Sylvia on anything like a permanent basis, I suggest you stay in your hutch and keep your inquisitive little whiskers out of my business. (*She starts to sweep out when she notices the expressions on the audience's faces—so she addresses them*) And you lot can shut up as well!

Daphne (*dejectedly*) This was going to be the most exciting thing that 'ad ever happened to me.

Sheba (*calling*) Come along, Joe! There's no time to dally!

Sheba exits

Joe (*shouting back*) Oh all right! (*To Daphne*) Sorry about this, Cinderella.

Daphne That's all right, Joe. I'm used to being ignored. I mean, most women think I'm a bloke and most blokes—think I'm a bloke.

Joe Leave it with me, Daph, I'll see what I can do.

Daphne Thanks, Joe. See yer.

Joe See yer, Daph.

Joe exits

The Lights fade. There is a magical feeling

Daphne Punctured football! (*She looks in a little mirror*) I don't know though.

(*Speaking*)   You know I've tried all the ointments
              The oils and the creams
              I've had all the ugly lumps
              Pampered and preened
              I've tried lotions and perfumes
              Exotic shampoos
              I've even had little bits
              Stuck on wiv glue
              If only some of my dreams would come right
              And some of my dreams
              Come true ...

Spotlight Daphne

Song 11: Believe in Fairies

When I was little
A wee tiny tot
I used to read stories
I read'em a lot
All about giants
And dragons and kings
Wizards and witches
And beautiful queens

My favourite one
Was about Cinderella
So pretty and perfect
Didn't look like a fella
Lovely and pure
Stacked with allure
Who went to the golden ball.

The fairies enter with a fur coat and a pair of high heeled shoes
This whole sequence should be like a ballet

Fairies Daphne Daphne
Just you believe
Believe in the fairies
And you will see
All of your wishes
They will come true
They will come true for you.

Daphne (*speaking*) Oh my Gawd. What's happenin'?

Fairies Daphne Daphne
Here is your gown

The fairies put a fur coat around Daphne

Handstitched already
For just fifty pound
All nicely tailored
Just feel the cloth
All guaranteed
Against mange and the moth.

Daphne (*speaking*) It's lovely. Really lovely!

Fairies Daphne Daphne
Boots for your feet

The fairies slip off her grotty flatties and put glittery high heels on Daphne

Dainty size eightsies
To make you complete
Once at the ball
How you'll flitter and flutter
Dressed to the nines
In your fairyland schmutter.

Daphne (*spoken*) Thank you very much but I must have something to take me there. Like a coach.

Fairies Daphne Daphne
What a to do
Asking for transport
Already are you

Act II   55

> Think of the overheads
> Think of the price
> A smart fairy cycle
> Would be very nice.

A huge rabbit—a magic rabbit like Bugs Bunny—enters, riding a tricycle—the bigger the cycle the better. Inside the rabbit skin is Joe Rabbit

Magic Rabbit (*cycling round the arena*)
> Daphne Daphne
> Just you believe
> Believe in the fairies
> And you will see
> You'll have a bicycle
> Just made for two
> Just made for two
> For you.

Daphne (*spoken*) It's smashin' and what a smart driver!

Daphne climbs on the back of the bike and they circle the area

All
> Daphne Daphne
> Just you believe
> Believe in the fairies
> And you will see
> All of your wishes
> They will come true
> They will come true for you.

The fairies all wave to Daphne

Joe stops the tricycle

Daphne 'Ere who is that under there? (*Pointing to the Rabbit's head*) Is that you, Joe Rabbit?
Joe (*taking off the Rabbit's head*) Yeah, magic, init!

Suddenly the Lights dim and swirl

Daphne whirls CS *as if blown by the wind*

Music: 11a

Joe exits, cycling

The fairies circle faster and faster round Daphne and the Lights fade

The Lights come up to show the City team, minus Joe, spinning round Daphne

Titch It's Daphne!

They all slow down and stop

All Hallo Daph!

Daphne Hallo.
Tubs You look really great, Daph!
Daphne Thanks, Tubs.
Lofty And you've arrived just in time to help us with the TV Special.
Daphne Oooo, can I?
Shaky Course, Daph. You'll add a bit of ker—ker—class.
Daphne You are nice, Shaky.
Einstein You look all funny and pale, Daphne.
Daphne I'm not surprised. Enid, you didn't, by any chance, see about half a dozen fairies running across the pitch, did you?
Enid I should be so lucky.
Daphne Then I must 'ave been dreaming.

The TV Floor Manager bursts in. He is very flamboyant and carries a clipboard and pencil. The TV camera operator and a camera on wheels enters, following

The groundstaff enter and set dressing-room benches and pegs. They exit

TV Floor Manager Girls! Girls! Can we please have some co-operation. We have already been rehearsing for over five hours and quite honestly I—am—limp!
Enid I know how you feel, love.
TV Floor Manager (*spotting Daphne*) What is that thing doing here?
Titch She's our mascot.
TV Floor Manager Oh very well, but keep it out of camera shot. Now we are going to record the short jingle first and then—we'll do the Club Song in the dressing room. This will be the final take. All right men?
All (*in incredibly deep voices*) Right. (*They assemble in a tight group by the already set dressing-room benches and pegs*)
TV Floor Manager Fab. Yar. Zowee. Camera! (*He points with his pencil*) Lights! (*He points with his pencil*) Action!

The TV Floor Manager points as:

The commentator enters

Commentator The Golden Ball Advertising Agency proudly presents a TV Soccer Special—"CITY. My City".
TV Floor Manager Cue Jingle. (*He points at the City team*)

Song 11b: City's are Red

City team (*hiding Daphne*) City's are red
United's are blue
What colour's yours?

They all duck down to reveal Daphne

Daphne   I'm not telling you.
TV Floor Manager (*appealing to the audience*) Why me? Why me!? Look, petals, we are going to do the song and then all go home. Yar?

Act II

All (*in incredibly deep voices again*) Yar.
TV Floor Manager Fab. Zowee. Camera! (*He points with his pencil*) Lights! (*He points with his pencil*) Action! (*He points at the Commentator*)
Commentator I'm standing here on the hallowed turf of the City Football Club. Scene of so many great matches. City Football Club. Where to be a 'man' is to be a City Player. Sheba Shekelstein, City's attractive mammoth—er—manager has successfully made players like Tubs!

Tubs waves

Enid!

Enid waves

Lofty!

Lofty waves

Titch!

The rest of the team lift Titch up and he waves

Shaky!

Lofty shines a torch towards the audience so that Shaky can see who to wave to

And Einstein!

Einstein turns with his back to the audience and waves

All of them—legends in their own minds.
TV Floor Manager Dialogue please. Keep it natural, petals. (*He points at the City team*)

During the following sequence the whole team suddenly become very puppet-like and are obviously terrified of the camera which they talk directly into regardless of where they are moving. They follow the camera with their heads and eyes

Lofty (*wiping his brow*) Whew! That—was—a—hard—session—lads.
City team (*wiping his brow; speaking in the same stilted fashion*) Whew! It—certainly—was—skipper.
Commentator What's that I hear. Could it be some of the merry badinage that typifies the fine spirit of this successful club. A club on its way to the pinnacle of soccer greatness. Whoops! Someone's left the dressing room door ajar—shall we listen in on the lads during one of their more informal moments. Shall we? Yes, let's. (*He swings open an imaginary door*)

The camera swoops down on the lads

Lofty (*looking at the camera*) Right—lads—you—have—done—jolly—well.
City team Thanks—skip! (*They all slap their thighs together as if rehearsed*)
Titch (*pushing to the front and talking directly to camera*) Hey, why—don't we—finish—off—with—the—old—club—song?
Lofty What—a—good—idea—young—Titch. Ah, here—comes—our—

star—Joe Rabbit—with—the—song-sheets. (*They all point away from Joe's entrance point still looking at the camera*)

Joe enters at a normal speed until he sees the camera

Joe (*carrying the song sheets*) Hallo, lads. Sorry I missed the training session——

The camera moves in on him

(*adopting a stilted manner*)—but—I—was—putting—the—finishing—touches—to—the—song—that—will—help—us—to—win—the—World—(*He hands out the sheets but looks at the camera*)

The team take the sheets looking at the camera

Cup.
Enid Is—it—romantic?
Joe Well—Enid—in—a—kind—of—way—it—is.
Shaky I hope it's not too fer fer fast.
Joe Here, Einstein (*he holds out a sheet marked 'music' in front of Einstein's eyes*) Can—you—read—music?
Einstein No. I—can—only—read—four—letter—words, but "I can kick it, stick it, whack it, crack it. Smack it in the back of the net"!
TV Floor Manager Cue song!

A song and dance routine follows

Song 12: Smack it in the Back of the Net

City team and the
TV Floor Manager
Down the City football club
Any day or night
You'll see us lads all training
Until we get it right
Sweating buckets
Dripping blood
Running ragged
Caked in mud
Making sure we're fit to win the cup.

City on the bubble
City on the move
City on the dribble
City in the groove
Git down 'ere, support us
You ain't seen nuffin' yet
See the crowd go crazy
When we smack it in the net.
When we stick it, kick it
Crack it, whack it
Smack it in the back of the net!

The opposition girls enter, running and join in the song and dance routine

Act II

Repeat verse

City team, TV Floor Manager and the **opposition girls**	City on the bubble City on the move City on the dribble City in the groove Git down 'ere, support us You ain't seen nuffin' yet See the crowd go crazy When we smack it in the net When we boot it, shoot it Sock it, knock it Stick it, kick it Pelt it, belt it Wang it, bang it Crack it in the back of the Whack it in the back of the Smack it in the back of the net. Goal!

Benny bursts in with Sylvia

Benny Stop the recording!

Daphne gets out her notebook and writes down the following

Sylv Cut the cameras!
TV Floor Manager Oh for heaven's sake!

The TV Floor Manager exits

Joe What's up Sylv? You look like you've just seen the *Sound of Music*.
Sylv Worse.
City team Worse?
Benny Worse.
Joe What is it?
Sylv They're at it!
City team At it?
Benny All over the dance floor.
Joe All over the d—— Daphne steady down—the rate you're goin' that bleedin' pencil'll catch fire. Now who's all over the dance floor?
Benny My Sheba and Norbert at the Flamenco da Gropa.
Sylv Dancing.
Benny Cheek to cheek.
Sylv And they wasn't face to face either. I had to cover Gazza's eyes.
Joe I'm not surprised.
Daphne (*relishing the scandal*) It's disgustin'
Benny She promised me she'd never be unfaithful, again.
Sylv She's gone too far this time.
Joe Right lads you get all the gear ready for Mexico, while we get down to that ballroom and save Norbert's honour.

Lofty And Benny's good name.

Joe Right.

They all exit, except Daphne

Daphne (*staying to confide with the audience*) It's disgustin'!

Daphne exits

The Lights fade to Black-out

During the Black-out the groundstaff set a garish free-standing archway displaying the words "Flamenco da Gropa". A glitter drape hangs down covering the entrance

When the Lights come up they are pink and there is a glitter-ball spinning

Ballroom music

The dance couples enter. They are dressed like "Come Dancing", with the men in monkey suits and the girls in tulle

The compere enters through the drape. He is followed by a spotlight

A fanfare interrupts the music at each of the following asterisks

Music: 12a

Compere Hallo and welcome. The Flamenco da Gropa is proud to present the final round of the coveted Romford and District "Waltzer of the Year" trophy. Let me present our six lovely finalists. Couple number one from Walthamstow—Elspeth and Reginald Problem!*

There is applause off stage as:

Elspeth and Reginald flounce forward. They are both bandy-legged

Elspeth hopes one day to own her own beauty salon while Reginald names his hobbies as road safety and adultery. Couple number two are Olga and Norman Strain from Bermondsey!*

There is applause from off stage as:

Olga and Norman step forward. They have very stiff legs and appear to find it difficult to bend, especially Olga

Olga's first love is amateur dramatics and excessive drinking. And finally tonight's hot favourite to win the title—recent winners in the "Andrews Liver Salts Open Tango"—may I give you Rachel Spubes and Alec Allcock of Ipswich!*

There is great applause from off stage

Rachel and Alec dance forward

If they win tonight's cash prize Rachel hopes to become a missionary in Majorca while Alec hopes to have enough money to complete his homemade electric organ. So here are the lucky couples dancing to a

Act II

number especially written for the occasion by our lovely hostess, Sheba Shekelstein—"The Valse Shekelstein" played tonight by Greg Griggs and the Groovy Groovers!

The dancing couples take their places as:

A small group of singers enter and take up their place in a corner of the ballroom. They are very old and look like Hinge and Bracket. The dance should be choreographed to include as much funny business as possible yet retaining the tempo and style of the waltz

Song 13: The Valse Shekelstein

Singers   From the Roxy in Romford
To the Mecca in Cheam
At the Starlight Assembly Rooms
Islington Green
They're swirling and twirling
In satin and sheen
They're dancing
The Valse Shekelstein.

Dancing dancing
Tinsel and tulle
Whirling whirling
Mad reckless fools
Feeling quite giddy
Dropping their jewels
All being sick in the main vestibule
Still swirling and twirling
In satin and sheen
They're dancing
The Valse Shekelstein.

Couple one—hoping that they'll catch the eye
Couple two—knowing it's now do or die
Couple three—sticking out front and behind
Completely blotto
Stoned out of their minds.
Drifting drifting
Fixed in a grin
Floating floating
Too many gins
Glitter of lipstick
Sparkle and spin
Praying to God
That their teeth'll stay in
They're swirling and twirling
In satin and sheen
They're dancing
The Valse Shekelstein.

The dancers finish up on the floor, remonstrating with each other

Compere And now as our lucky couples clear the floor and our judges have the difficult task of making their final decisions—we bring you a surprise high spot to the evening. Our lovely hostess Sheba Shekelstein has agreed to take the floor herself accompanied by her new escort, Norbert Brando. Hold your breath as they dance the sensuous Jezebel Tango.

Music 13b: The Jezebel Tango

Norbert appears in the spot. He is wearing a bright red frilly shirt, tight black Spanish trousers, and has a red rose in his mouth. He would, in fact look quite macho but for the fact that he has still got his flat cap on

Sheba enters wearing a revealing one-piece Spanish dress

The dance steps of Sheba will be perfect and Norbert is surprisingly good but he does tend to get chucked about by Sheba. The dance needs to be short and funny ending with Sheba sweeping off Norbert's hat, throwing away the rose and kissing him just as:

Benny and Joe enter

Benny Stop all here, right now and this!
Joe Try again, Benny.
Benny What? Oh yeah. Stop all this, right here and now!
Joe That's better.

Sylv and Daphne enter with some suitcases

Sheba Benjamin, how dare you! Have you completely lost your toupee?

The singers, dancers and compere exit, realizing a 'situation' has arisen

Benny Silence—Jezebel!

Everyone, apart from Benny, gasps

Joe Well done Benny.
Norbert I'm sorry Mr Shekelstein.
Benny You've nothing to be sorry for, Norbert. You were lured!
Norbert "Lured"?
Benny Lured. You've been her little plaything!
Sylv Her little toy.
Daphne Her little bit on the side.
Joe Shut up, Daphne.
Daphne Sorry.
Benny You're not the first, Norbert, but you're going to be the last.
Sheba What are you going to do, Benjamin?
Benny *(losing his courage)* I'll tell you what I'm—going—to do ...
Sylv Don't falter, Father.
Benny I'm going to make some changes.
Sheba Oh yes?

Act II

Benny (*screwing up his eyes*) Yes. From now on I'm going to wear the knickers in this outfit.
All (*apart from Sheba*) YES!
Sheba (*shaken*) You're serious.
Joe Course he's serious. Look his eyes are all screwed up.
Benny (*still with his eyes screwed up*) Are they?
Joe Yeah.
Benny Oh yeah so they are.
Sheba What are you telling me, Benjamin.
Benny I'm telling you that you're all washed up.
Sheba I just asked.
Benny I just answered.
All (*apart from Sheba*) YES!!!
Benny Sheba, I'm going to take back our wedding ring and I'll only return it when you can learn to act like my wife.

Sheba returns the ring

No more nagging.
Norbert No more Norbert.
Sylv No more nookie.
Joe Shut up, Sylv.
Sylv Sorry.
Benny What do you say to that?

Sheba moves to one end of the area

Everyone else forms a small group at the other end

Song 14: Forgive Me Already

Sheba (*near to tears*) What can I say?
What can I do?
Forgive me
I've dallied with too many men
When I loved only you, my Ben
Forgive me.
I'll go down on my knees and say
No more strife
My life, oi vey.
I'll promise that I'll never lie
Cross my heart and hope to die
Forgive me
Already.

Humility
Timidity
You want that I should learn
All right then
Obedience
Subservience

> You want that I should have
> I'll try then
> So much I'm hoping
> To prove my worth
> Just as I promised
> For better or worse
> So whether you're healthy or whether you're ill
> All I ask Benjamin
> Is
> Don't change your will!
>
> What can I say?
> What can I do?
> Forgive me.
> I've dallied with too many men
> When I loved only you, my Ben
> Forgive me
> I'll go down on my knees and say
> No more strife
> My life, oi vey!
> I'll promise that I'll never lie
> Cross my heart, hope to die
> Forgive me
> Forever and ever
> Already.

At the end of the song they are all blubbering

Sheba (*sniffing*) Can you ever find it in your heart to forgive me, Bennikins?
Joe (*blubbering*) Can we ever find it in our hearts to forgive her, Bennikins?
Benny (*suddenly stops blubbering*) Certainly not.
All (*stopping instantly as well*) No, certainly not.
Benny How could you, Sheba. Only minutes before we set off to Mexico for the World Cup.
Sylv Everything we've been working for.
Daphne Upsetting the team. You're disgustin'.
Sheba Yes, you're right. Benjamin.

They all look at Benjamin

> (*Putting out her hand*) Fingers!

Benny smacks her hand for being naughty

Joe Well, it's no good standing here all night being sorry. We've got a cup to win, right?
All Right.
Benny So watch out Mexico.

The men offer their arms to the girls

> We're on our way!

Act II 65

Music: 14a

Norbert, Joe, Daphne and Sylv sweep off

Benny (*gently*) Sheba.
Sheba (*like a pussy cat*) Yes, pumpkin?
Benny (*dominantly*) The bags! (*He points to a pile of suitcases*)
Sheba (*subserviently*) Yes, pumpkin.

Sheba runs and collects all the cases as:

Benny exits

Sheba follows behind then halfway across the area she stops

(*Telling the audience*) Course, it'll never last!

Sheba exits

There is the sound of Mexican peasants as they stream onto the area. They are noisy, excited and continually make Mexican noises accompanied by 'cod' Mexican expressions. They all wear battered hats, old loose shirts and three quarter length trousers. The hullabaloo is brought to a halt by the gun fired by Right Hand Hombre

Right Hand Hombre (*standing on a raised block or the backs of peasants*) Hombres, pleeze, silencios for your pre-si-den-tey. Hosay Hooleeho Hasta la Vista Tequila.
Hombres (*clapping with each syllable*) Pre-si-den-tey! Pre-si-den-tey! Pre-si-den-tey!

A spotlight picks up the Presidente. He may either stride in but it is funnier if he is inside a small mock-up tank. He wears a bogus military uniform and masses of medals. He enters with arm in the Fascist salute but when he salutes the crowd and audience he has a silly salute where the thumb of the saluting hand gets repeatedly caught in his nostril

Presidente Hombres. I—Hosay Hooleho Hasta la Vista Tequila, Presidentey of all Meh—

The Presidente's voice always sticks on this word and he cannot say the rest until the Right Hand Hombre relieves the 'blockage' with a throat-spray squirt

—hico, welcome our World Cup team—Chi Hua Hua H'Academicalez.
Hombres (*chanting as the team runs in*) Chi Hua Hua. Chi Hua Hua. Chi Hua Hua!

The Mexican team enter, running. They line up—they are not in soccer kit but big Mexican hats

Presidente Theez team make terrible meestake. Lasta week they lose to team from H'Argentina.
Hombres (*shocked*) H'Argentina?
Presidente Si. H'and theez is their rewards. Ready!

The Hombres kneel

The Mexican team stand with their knees shaking

Aim.

The Hombres raise imaginary guns and the team put their hands up

Fire!

The Hombres go 'bang'

The team screams then throw themselves up in the air before falling to the ground. They each have a leg or arm sticking up

Now no one from H'Argentina will be able to laugh again at footballers from Meh—

When the Right Hand Hombre squirts the Presidente's throat the legs and arms of the team collapse

-hico!

Hombres (*clapping and chanting*) Pre-si-den-tey! Pres-si-den-tey! Pre-si-den-tey!

Presidente Remove these traitors from my sight!

The Presidente and the Hombres all put their hands over their eyes as:

The team comes to life, bows to the audience and scarpers

The others remove their hands from their eyes

Thatsa better. Never again will zey betray us.

Right Hand Hombre But Presidente, who will play against zee gringos of Ceety Football Club, now that all zee players are dead?

Presidente No problos. I—Presidentey——

Hombres }
Presidente } (*chanting; together*) Hosay Hooleho Hasta la Vista Tequila— have found a new team.

Right Hand Hombre A new team?

Presidente Si! A new team formed from my personal bodyguard. H'everyone of them is a trained killer and bandito.

Right Hand Hombre A brillios idea, Presidente.

Presidente H'of coursios. And here they are ... Goalkeeper, Boleros Giganticus!

Hombres (*shouting*) Ole!

Boleros Giganticus enters, carrying two footballs under her jumper

Presidente Defences—Tijuana Brasso!

Tijuana Brasso enters, shaking maracas

Hombres Ole!

Presidente H'and Nasty Juarez!

Nasty Juarez enters, scratching an itch

Hombres Ole!

Presidente Midfield. Midios D'Alfafa!

Act II

Midios D'Alfafa enters, blowing a big kiss
Hombres Ole!
Presidente Attack. Grandios Moustachios!
Grandios Moustachios enters, twirling her big moustache
Hombres Ole!
Presidente And ze greatest player in all Meh—
The Right Hand Hombre squirts the Presidente's throat
-hico!
Hombres No!
Presidente Si! *Big Maracas*!!
Hombres Oooooooooolllllllllllleeeeeeeeeee!

The Hombres make more noise than ever as they run to their places for the song and dance

> *When Big Maracas enters, he is carried in by four Hombres on a highly decorated litter. He is dressed in the most outrageously colourful outfit with silver lamé shorts and silver football boots. The colours are hideous. He has the biggest Mexican sombrero you have ever seen and a long drooping black moustache. He throws rose petals and flowers to the audience on his royal procession around the area*

In the dance the scenes in the verses should be acted out

The Hombres can play guitars

Song 15: Big Maracas

Hombres	Big Maracas
	Aye yi yi
	Big Maracas
	My my my
	He h'okay
	He h'all right
	Big Maracas he dynamite.
Presidente	Now all you Hombres
	Hear my song
	It's very leetle
	And won't take long
	It's all about
	Our hero man
	called Big Maracas
	The football man.
	Some bandits come to Vera Cruz
	Full of tequila, full of booze
	Shoot the Sheriff, shoot his son
	Till Big Maracas kick their bum.
	I buy a pony

Hombres
Got no skin
Feel so boney
Feel so thin
But "BM" say
At half past nine
squeeze his maracas
And he'll be fine.
Big Maracas
Aye yi yi
Big Maracas
My my my
He h'okay
He h'all right
Big Maracas
He dynamite

At the end of the song the Presidente holds up his hands for silence

Presidente Caballeros. If you win zee World Cup today, you will receive from the Republic of Meh—

The Right Hand Hombre squirts the Presidente's throat

—hico—

They all lean forward with expectancy

—one season ticket for "Disneyland!"
Hombres Carrrramba!
Presidente But—if you fail then—poof! (*He demonstrates they will be shot*)
Hombres Muchos Gracias, Presidente. It will be an honour to die.
Presidente Now for the big match against zee gringos and adios to Sheba Shekelstos!
Hombres Ole!
Presidente Vamoos!

Everyone exits in a flash accompanied by Mexican sound effects, except the Presidente

Sheba and Benny enter, obviously talking about the Presidente

Sheba Oh I don't know, I rather like the President. He's the sort of hombre that could grow on you.
Benny Yeah, like warts.
Presidente Ah—Senorita Shekelstos. Welcome to Meh——
Benny Atishoo!
Presidente Hico. (*To Benny*) Muchos Gracias.
Benny My pleasure.
Presidente I feel so sorry for your team.
Sheba Sorry?
Presidente Si. We have learned ze very latest football techniques from H'England. Techniques that will defeat you.
Benny What techniques?

Act II

Presidente Oh come, Señor, don't be so naïve. I'm talking about your famous hokey-cokey methodos.
Sheba Great Neasden!
Benny He knows! The lads won't stand a chance.
Presidente Let the game begeen!

The Hombres, who are now the Chi Hua Hua supporters enter and take up their places

Norbert, Daphne and Sylv enter and join Sheba and Benny on the other side

Speakos di loudos Welcome Presidente, señors, señoritas and underprivileged hombres. Welcome to the Stadios Aztec for the World Cup Final. And now pleez give a warm Mexican welcome to those feelthy English pigs—City Football Club.
Hombres Boo!

The City team enter

Speakos di loudos And our own Mexican Jumping beans—Chi Hua Hua Academicalez!
Hombres (*with a tremendous chant*) Chi Hua Hua! Chi Hua Hua! Chi Hua Hua!

The Chi Hua Hua team enter and jump about like beans, except for the cool Maracas

The referee enters with a football and starts blowing his whistle as:

The two teams line up

Referee (*placing the ball down on the centre spot*) Right gentlemen zis time vee get it right. Ja?
All Ja!
Referee Very vell. Prepare for kick off. (*He blows the whistle*)

The teams go into slow motion, as the City players take a swing at the Chi Hua Hua players who duck and dish out the hokey-cokey routine

Song 15a: Hokey Cokey

Chi Hua Hua   You put zee left muchacha in
　　　　　　　　Zee left muchacha out
　　　　　　　　In out, in out
　　　　　　　　You boot 'em all about
　　　　　　　　You do the bossa nova
　　　　　　　　And then vamoose quick
　　　　　　　　Cos zat's what its all about!
　　　　　　　　Ole!

The City players are left writhing on the pitch

Referee (*blowing his whistle*) Half time!

Music: 15b

The Hombre Supporters, Presidente, Right Hand Hombre and the Chi Hua Hua team all freeze

There is a moment of silence as:

The City team sort themselves out. They clutch various injuries

This freeze must be held through the ensuing dialogue

Sheba (*running down to the players*) Benjamin, what can we do?
Lofty It was a massacre, Mrs S.
Enid I couldn't bear to watch.
Shaky My shin bone's completely fer—fer—fer—bruised.
Joe My ankle's a write-off.
Sylv We can't go on two short in the second half.
Daphne What about Tubs?
Sheba Tubs is still on suspension.
Tubs Worse luck.
Benny Well where are we going to suddenly find two players, dedicated enough to sacrifice themselves for the sake of City?

Mrs Brillo and Mrs Rinse enter running, dressed in City football gear, still wearing headscarves

Mrs Rinse
Mrs Brillo } (*together*) We're ready for the call, Mr Shekelstein.
Sheba Oh No!
Benny Oh yes! Do you think you can do it?
Mrs Rinse
Mrs Brillo } (*together*) Course we can. (*They bend down to do up their laces*)
Benny (*patting their bottoms*) That's my girls!
Sheba Benjamin!

They all look at him

Fingers!
Benny (*whipping away his hands*) Sorry dear.
Referee (*coming to life and blowing his whistle*) Second half! Change ends!

The scene comes to action as the freeze ends and the teams change ends

Shaky's place is taken by Mrs Rinse and Joe's by Mrs Brillo

Forty five minutes remaining! (*He blows his whistle for the start*)
Lofty (*shouting*) Let us pray!

Immediately all the Chi Hua Hua team fall to their knees and start to cross themselves, finger their rosaries, do 'Hail Marys' etc

Mrs Brillo dribbles the ball towards the goal. She stops

They stop praying. It's too late to do anything—they join in with the ensuing dialogue

Act II

Mrs Brillo Hildegard's got the ball. (*She puts her foot on it*)
All (*whispering*) Hildegard's got the ball.
Mrs Brillo Hildegard's going to shoot. (*She puts her foot back*)
All (*whispering*) Hildegard's going to shoot.
Mrs Brillo Hildegard's shot! (*She hits the ball in the back of the net*)

Mrs Rinse jumps up and her shorts fall round her ankles

All GOAL!

The City team rush to Mrs Brillo to congratulate her

The Referee blows a long blast on his whistle and there is absolute silence!

All look at the Referee who slowly walks towards Mrs Rinse and points at her fallen shorts

Referee Indecent exposure!

All gasp

Penalty!

Big Maracas picks up the ball and walks towards the penalty spot

Hombres Big Ma—ra—cas! Big Ma—ra—cas! Big Ma—ra—cas!

Big Maracas places the ball as:

Mrs Rinse pulls up her shorts and there is a second freeze where only the speakers move

Daphne If he scores this penalty we've lost. If only we could've held out.
Sheba We're finished.
Presidente The whole of Meh—

The Right Hand Hombre squirts the Presidente's throat

hico is watching you, Maracas.
Sylv What we need now is a miracle.
Presidente If you believe in miracles, amigos, you'll believe in anything.
Daphne "Wait a minute!"

A spot narrows down on Daphne as the stage lights fade

The fairies enter in the other spot

Music: 15c

There is total stillness

Song 16: Believe in Fairies (Reprise)

Fairies   Daphne Daphne
              Just you believe
              Use little Gazzie
              To nibble his knee

> All of your wishes
> They can come true
> They can come true
> For you.

The stage lights come up as:

The fairies disappear

Daphne That's it. Use Gazza, Sylv. He'd be up his shorts before you could say——

Sylv Maracas?

Daphne Exactly.

Sylv Go on Gazzie, you can do it. For the sake of City.

There is a drum roll and during the following speech the spotlight which represents Gazza circles the auditorium. The spot is small but bright

The crowd start to whisper "Gazza! Gazza! Gazza!" which builds in urgency as the spotlight gets closer to Maracas' shorts

Music: 16a

Maracas (*oblivious to the spot circling the walls*) Big Maracas he got the ball. (*He puts his foot on it*) Big Maracas he going to shoot (*He lifts his foot up*) Big Maracas he——

The spot shoots up Maracas' leg, to the sound of Swanee whistle, and goes out

Aaaiiieeeooouuu!

Maracas mis-hits the ball which goes past the goal and he clutches his shorts

The Hombres throw up their hats etc.

The City team congratulate each other, especially Mrs Brillo

Referee (*blowing his whistle*) Full time. The winner of the Verld Cup. City Football Club!

One of the groundstaff brings in the cup and hands it to Mrs Brillo, who holds it aloft

There is a terrific cheer

The whole team assemble with the management for a quick flash photograph taken by the referee

Presidente Very well, Señora Shekelstos. Zis time you win zee cup but next time, just wait and see. Now for the rewards I promise my team— (*addressing the Hombres*) I Presidentey Hosay Hooleho Hasta la Vista Tequila never forget a debt.

The Mexican team fall to their knees

Ready! Aim!

Act II

The Hombres turn their imaginary guns on the Presidente
   Fire!
They shoot the Presidente
Right Hand Hombre We are free!
Hombres Viva Zapata!
Right Hand Hombre Who shall we choose as our new Presidente?
Hombres Big Maracas! Big Maracas! Big Maracas!
Right Hand Hombre (*twirling his imaginary gun*) Long live the Presidente. (*He fires it*) Santa Maria, I've just keeled myself. (*He drops and dies*)
Hombres Ole!

The Hombres and the Mexican team exit with Big Maracas

Benny Well, what an end to the season.
Joe Well done, Benny.
Titch And Gazzie.
Tubs Right.
Shaky Hadn't we better go and fer—fer—fer—find him?
Lofty Quick as a flash as always Shaky. Come on lads. You never know we might need Gazzie for next season!

The City team exits, except Joe

Sheba Although it's the end of the season, Benny, could there possibly be a new beginning for you and I?
Benny No more arguments?
Sheba No more arguments.
Benny I make all the decisions.
Sheba You make all the decisions.
Norbert Well, Benny?
Benny I don't know what to do.
Sheba How about, Benjamin ...

They all look at him

   Finger? (*She extends the ring finger of her left hand*)
Benny Why not? (*He slips the wedding ring back on her finger*)
Sylv Joe.

They all look at him

   Finger? (*She extends her hand likewise*)
Joe Blimey this is catching. (*He slips a ring on her finger*)
Daphne Norbert?

They all look at him

   We'd better get this cup back to the City supporters.
Norbert Thank gawd for that!

The City supporters stream onto the area and parade Benny with the cup around the arena

Song 17: Finale

Supporters Wot a day
City's gone and done it
Wot a day
We've gone and won the cup, cup, cup
Wot a day
We really can't believe it
Now after three
The booze'll be free
And all the pubs will give away grub!
Birds up the manor'll
Cost only a tanner
The world's gone bleedin' mad
So give a cheer
For Benny and beer
And the city we love
City we love
City we love
Best!
Oi!

The principal actors exit and return to take their curtain call during the following

(*Clap-clap: clap-clap-clap: clap-clap-clap-clap!*) City!
(*Clap-clap: clap-clap-clap: clap-clap-clap-clap!*) City!
(*Clap-clap: clap-clap-clap: clap-clap-clap-clap!*) City!

Song 18: City (Reprise)

Supporters City! City!
Isn't it a pity
You can't tell
Yer left foot from yer right
Yer shootin's hit and miss
'Arf the time yer Brahms and Liszt
And yer haven't scored a goal
Fer sixteen weeks.
City! City!
Where's yer nitty gritty
You must really try and give it some
Start dishin' out the dirties
Hack their shins and rip their shirties
Jist get us off the bottom of the league
But we'll support yer
And stick by yer
We will wear the red and white
Though the full backs are both toothless
And the midfield's bleedin' useless

Act II 75

>They 'ave never let us down
> So when Saturday comes round
> We'll be out there in the crowd
> Singin', "City we luv you"
> City! City!
> Isn't it a pity
> Isn't it a pity
> We luv you!

The Company exits to the rhythmic clap—when the stage is empty the Fairies dressed in football gear place a hamster cage containing live Gazza Hamster on the centre spot. The cage bears a sign "Our Hero"

CURTAIN

FURNITURE AND PROPERTY LIST

ACT I

On stage: Goalposts

Off stage: Stretchers with velcro strips **(St John's Ambulance)**
Large pad, pencil **(Daphne)**
Table. *Under it:* shelf. *On it:* box marked sound effects with large red button on it **(Two groundstaff)**
Four chairs **(Four groundstaff)**
Baby's feeding bottles, blankets **(Police and groundstaff)**
Tea-trolley. *On it:* urn, cups, saucers, one biscuit, teaspoons, washing-up liquid **(Joe)**
Football **(Norbert)**
Trolley. *On it:* working tape recorder **(Einstein)**
Six towels, six chairs, six watering cans painted in city colours. *In them:* warm water **(Shower girls)**
City F.C. refuse bag **(Mrs Brillo and Mrs Rinse)**
Chaise longue/settee **(Groundstaff)**
Lampstand **(Groundstaff)**
Table: *On it:* white cloth, two full glasses, ice bucket. *In it:* opened bottle of champagne. Plate. *On it:* cheese and pineapple sticks, sausage sticks etc **(Groundstaff)**
Huge perfume spray **(Sheba)**
Newspapers and magazines **(Daphne)**
Travel bags etc **(City team and the management)**
Football **(Herr Vistlekraut)**

Personal: **Shaky:** white stick, dark glasses
Sylv: bottle of nail varnish, "hamster"
Daphne: crumpled piece of toilet paper, glasses
Sheba: glasses, wedding ring, sweatband
Einstein: watch
Mrs Rinse: tablets, headscarf
Norbert: flat cap, contract
Mrs Brillo: headscarf
Referee: whistle, 'Adolf Hitler' moustache
Shower girls: shower caps

ACT II

On stage: Raised block. *On it:* Queen's seat
Goalposts

Off stage: Royal corgi **(Queen)**
Tea trolley. *On it:* ice-bucket. *In it:* bottle of almost empty champagne.

Five glasses. *In them:* champagne. Empty glasses, white cloth, three
bouquets **(Mrs Rinse and Mrs Brillo)**
Fur coat, high heeled pair of shoes **(Fairies)**
Tricycle **(Joe)**
Camera **(Operator)**
Benches and coat pegs **(Groundstaff)**
Torch **(Lofty)**
Song sheets marked "Music" **(Joe)**
Tank **(Presidente)**
Hamster cage with sign **(Fairies)**

Personal: **Norbert:** trimphone
Daphne: little mirror
Mexican team: big Mexican hats, rosaries
Big Maracas: large hat, large drooping moustache
Grandios Moustachios: moustache
Benny: rings
Boleros Giganticus: two footballs
Right-hand Hombre: throat-spray, gun
City Staff: World Cup
Joe: ring

LIGHTING PLOT

Property fittings required: working lamp
Exterior and interior

ACT I. Afternoon

To open: Bright, general afternoon effect

| Cue 1 | **Butcher** has the ball in front of the city goal
Lights dim slightly | (Page 3) |

| Cue 2 | A great fountain of water squirts upwards and down on **Joe** and **Sylv**
Lights fade to Black-out and then come up brightly | (Page 15) |

| Cue 3 | There is a reprise of the last chorus and they finish up collapsed in the two chairs
Black-out and then the Lights come up pink and seductive. As the Lights come up the lamp comes on | (Page 27) |

| Cue 4 | **Joe:** "Oh no!"
Black-out, including the lamp | (Page 33) |

| Cue 5 | **Sylv** and **Joe** exit with the settee and the lamp
Lights come up as floodlights | (Page 33) |

| Cue 6 | The sound of the plane taking off
Lights fade to darkness | (Page 37) |

| Cue 7 | When ready
Lights come up to afternoon effect | (Page 37) |

| Cue 8 | At the end of Song 9
House lights come up | (Page 42) |

ACT II

To open: Bright, sunny afternoon effect

| Cue 9 | **Joe** exits
Lights fade and become magical | (Page 53) |

| Cue 10 | **Daphne:** "Come true ..."
Spotlight **Daphne** | (Page 53) |

| Cue 11 | **Joe:** "Yeah, magic innit!"
Lights dim and swirl | (Page 55) |

| Cue 12 | **The Fairies** circle faster and faster round **Daphne**
Lights fade. When ready bring up bright interior effect | (Page 55) |

Cue 13	**Daphne** exits *Lights fade to Black-out*	(Page 60)
Cue 14	When ready *Pink lighting with a spot for the compere*	(Page 60)
Cue 15	**Compere:** "... Jezebel Tango." *Cut spot and bring up on Norbert*	(Page 62)
Cue 16	**Hombres:** "Pre-si-den-tey!" *Spotlight the President*	(Page 65)
Cue 17	**Daphne:** "Wait a minute!" *Spotlight narrows down on **Daphne** as the stage lights fade*	(Page 71)
Cue 18	**The Fairies** enter *Second spot*	(Page 71)
Cue 19	**The Fairies** disappear *Cut second spot and bring up the Lights as before*	(Page 72)
Cue 20	There is a drum roll *Small, bright spot circles the auditorium*	(Page 72)
Cue 21	**Maracas:** "Big Maracas he...." *Spot shoots up Maracas' leg and goes out*	(Page 72)
Cue 22	When the stage is empty *Centre spot*	(Page 75)

EFFECTS PLOT

ACT I

Cue 1	The Lights come up brightly *Cock crows*	(Page 15)
Cue 2	**Benny** presses down the red button *Sound of plane taking off*	(Page 37)

ACT II

Cue 3	Everyone exits in a flash, except the President *Mexican sound effects*	(Page 68)
Cue 4	The spot shoots up Maracas' leg *Swanee whistle*	(Page 72)

A licence issued by Samuel French Ltd to perform this play does NOT include permission to use any copyright music other than the published score in the performance. The notice printed below on behalf of the Performing Right Society should be carefully read.

The following statement concerning the use of music is printed here on behalf of the Performing Right Society Ltd, by whom it was supplied

The permission of the owner of the performing right in copyright music must be obtained before any public performance may be given, whether in conjunction with a play or sketch or otherwise, and this permission is just as necessary for amateur performances as for professional. The majority of copyright musical works (other than oratorios, musical plays and similar dramatico-musical works) are controlled in the British Commonwealth by the PERFORMING RIGHT SOCIETY LTD, 29-33 BERNERS STREET, LONDON W1P 4AA.

The Society's practice is to issue licences authorizing the use of its repertoire to the proprietors of premises at which music is publicly performed, or, alternatively, to the organizers of musical entertainments, but the Society does not require payment of fees by performers as such. Products or promotors of plays, sketches, etc., at which music is to be performed, during or after the play or sketch, should ascertain whether the premises at which their performances are to be given are covered by a licence issued by the Society, and if they are not, should make application to the Society for particulars as to the fee payable.

MADE AND PRINTED IN GREAT BRITAIN BY
LATIMER TREND & COMPANY LTD PLYMOUTH
MADE IN ENGLAND

www.ingramcontent.com/pod-product-compliance
Lightning Source LLC
LaVergne TN
LVHW051753080426
835511LV00018B/3310